PRAISE

for

Victorious Spiritual Warfare:
So Simple, Grandma Can Do It

I would like to offer a strong endorsement for Maureen Broderson's new book, "Victorious Spiritual Warfare." We live in a world that is so complex, so chaotic, and so broken, but we have often propped people up, and put bandaids on their injuries when nothing but spiritual surgery will bring healing and help. Maureen communicates a powerful message to liberate those trapped by their current journey. Many are unaware and her insightful teaching will bring light where there has been darkness, freedom where there has been bondage, and hope where there has been helplessness. She is an experienced practitioner and her words and counsel can be trusted!

GLENN BURRIS, Jr.
Former President of The Foursquare Church, US

Maureen Broderson has penned a timely new book on an often misunderstood subject, spiritual warfare. Her keen insight strips away the fog of confusion and brings into focus the all too real spiritual forces of evil who try to keep us bound from living the life God has prepared for us to live. Most importantly, she provides the reader a practical guide that shows, step by step, how to use the power that God has given us to defeat the enemy and to live a life of freedom and victory. Her book is clear, concise, and shows us that evil is powerless when the good are unafraid.

JIM GOSS, Sr. Vice President, INSP Creative Services,
On-Air Promotion, and Short Form Programming;
Director Creative Production & Promotion,
NBC Television Network, retired.

The topic of spiritual warfare often invites extremes—there are those who overdramatize it as well as those who ignore it, but neither path leads to the joyful freedom offered to every believer. I know Maureen Broderson as a Biblically faithful and balanced guide who has helped countless people in all kinds of churches, including the church I pastor, live in victory over the plans and the power of the enemy. I wholeheartedly recommend this book as a practical, easy-to-read road map to the freedom and fullness secured by Jesus.

TIM CLARK, Senior Pastor,
The Church On The Way, Van Nuys, California

Maureen Broderson may be an "ordinary grandma," but she has an unordinary grasp of the spiritual dimensions which surround us. Hers is not just "head knowledge" but practical, biblically sound knowledge of this spiritual dimension, where God wants His children to live victoriously.

In these pages and chapters, you will find biblical truths and spiritual principles to enable you to penetrate the realms of darkness, which may have oppressed you, and assist others in finding their own walk of spiritual freedom and victory.

GARY CURTIS, Staff Pastor,
The Church On The Way, Van Nuys, California, retired

Maureen Broderson takes the subject of "Spiritual Warfare" off the shelves of theology books and onto the coffee table of every believer. Her easy, understandable, and balanced communication of this oft-misunderstood part of the Christian life is encouraging and empowering.

SEAN APPLETON, Senior Pastor,
Hope Chapel, Lancaster, California

Clear, engaging, accessible. Those three words came to mind when I read Maureen Broderson's lucid and balanced guide to spiritual warfare. Readers will recognize themselves in her stories, and will be able to see themselves following the path that she lays out. These principles transcend cultural boundaries, as I have found them as effective in Vietnam and China as they are in my home church.

BRUCE GARNER, D.Min., M.Div.,
Missions Pastor, CenterPoint Church, Burton, MI

This is a fresh and compelling presentation on Spiritual Warfare that is solidly biblical, theologically sound, and validated by the author through decades of hands-on ministry to thousands of Believers.

As a powerful and highly motivating text, it calls ordinary Believers to action in the battle to defeat the personal and demeaning strategies and assaults Satan employs to destroy God's children. Highlighting the foundational truth that Jesus Christ has given every Believer His authority and His power to defeat the enemy and to receive healing and wholeness in every dimension of their lives, the author compels the readers to boldly use this God-given authority and power.

A must read, this volume presents readers with a spiritual empowerment experience that will transform their lives. It will inspire them to embrace the strength of the enablement of the Holy Spirit in their lives and provide the confidence and blueprint to become an effective warrior and victor over the assaults of Satan.

Readers will learn to hear the voice of God, embrace the active partnership of the Holy Spirit, and discover the freedom God has for their lives.

A powerfully strategic volume!

PAUL G. CHAPPELL, Ph.D.
Provost El Camino Christian College,
California Site Director, Randall University,

What you hold in your hands is the fruit of someone who has been pursuing Jesus wholeheartedly. What Maureen Broderson shares with us is out of the overflow of her faithful study of scripture and relationship with God. My prayer is that as you read this book that you wouldn't just be equipped, but that you would also draw closer to the living God.

REV. DR. DREW SAMS, Senior Pastor,
Bel Air Church, Los Angeles, CA

Do you ever feel like you are in a war you cannot win, one that you cannot see and yet experience its repercussions in your life, family, and community? There is good news! The spiritual war is real; but it's an already-been-won war! We can be victorious because Jesus is victorious.

Maureen encourages believers to live as everyday warriors of our King and His Kingdom, listening for our Father's voice, confidently standing in Christ's authority and power, willing to partner with the Holy Spirit in our continuing freedom and restoration and offering this same freedom to others. Through her conversational, pastoral style and practical examples, Maureen invites us on a scriptural journey with the Holy Spirit to trust, believe, and choose. She asks, "Are you ready to join the battle?

DR. LEAH COULTER, Ph.D.,
Director, *Mending Heart Ministries*,
Author, Adjunct Professor, Retired Pastor

This terrific book is an excellent introduction to spiritual warfare, and gives insight into the fight against the principalities and powers that limit our relationship with God and one another. Every layman and pastor will benefit from Maureen's experience.

DAVID J. WILSON, J.D.
Attorney, Author, Professor, Musician

Victorious
SPIRITUAL
WARFARE

So Simple, Grandma can do it!

MAUREEN A. BRODERSON

VIDE

Scripture quotations marked NLT are taken from the Holy Bible, New Living Translation, copyright ©1996, 2004, 2007, 2013 by Tyndale House Foundation. Used by permission of Tyndale House Publishers, Inc., Carol Stream, Illinois 60188. All rights reserved.

Scripture quotations marked NKJV are taken from the Holy Bible, New King James Version. Copyright ©1982 by Thomas Nelson, Inc., used by permission. All rights reserved.

Scripture quotations marked ESV are from the Holy Bible, English Standard Version, copyright ©2001 by Crossway Bibles, a division of Good News Publishers. Used by permission. All rights reserved.

Vide Press
6200 Second Street
Washington D.C. 20011
www.VidePress.com

ISBN: 978-1-954618-12-1 (Print)

Printed in the United States of America

Certification of Registration's: TXu 2-232-496, TXu 2-249-627

DEDICATION

Without ceasing, I will praise the goodness and faithfulness of God, and I dedicate this book to Him. Also, to all the "ordinary people," myself included, whom the Lord longs to empower and equip for the extraordinary things in life His love and victorious freedom promise.

ACKNOWLEDGMENTS

I've been taught one is too small of a number to accomplish anything big. In writing this book, I've once again discovered the truth of this statement. I am profoundly grateful to Tom Freiling, Director of Vide Press, and his professional team, who has helped shape my manuscript. They have given me a platform to share my story and offered stunning design and production to make this book possible. Jeffry Parker has been a particular source of ever-patient, expert assistance, and gracious support. Thank you, sir.

Many have encouraged me throughout my writing journey. First and foremost, I owe an enormous debt of gratitude to my family. Thank you to my faithful husband Lance, our daughters Kelly and Lori, their husbands Jeff and Brad, and our most amazing grandsons, Nicholas, Lucas, and Declan. I recognize each one of you as a glorious blessing from God's hand to my heart. Thank you for your love, prayerful support, and sacrificially taking care of so many of life's tasks to give me time and opportunity to disappear into our home office to write. This book would not have been possible without you.

Additionally, I'm overwhelmed with gratitude for the prayers, invaluable insights, expert guidance, and ongoing encouragement of Gary Curtis, David Wilson, Jim Goss, Dr. Robert Rohm, Bob Anderson, Dr. Paul Chappell, Dr. Leah Coulter, Michelle Glush, and Bob Goff.

These have faithfully partnered with a vast army of prayer warriors who have graciously come alongside me to see this book transition from a dream to reality. My heartfelt thanks go to Pastors Tim and Deborah Clark, Dan and Brenda Hicks, Elizabeth Ewens, Glenn and Debbie Burris, Jack and Valerie Hayford, Alisa Curtis, Carmen Quevedo, Jonathan Berglund, Courtney and Hazel Hall, Bruce and Sharon Garner, Sean and Kay Appleton, Dr. Drew Sams, Kyle and Teresa Bauer, Jeff and Cecilia Freeman, and Joy Dawson.

Joining with them to sustain me in prayer, I extend my humble thanks to Cheryl Goss, Marilyn Chappell, Joy Frey, Charlie Shaw, Martin and Bea Laufer, Jim and Debbie Schopper, Mike and Sandy Miller, Chris and Myrene Glass, Seth and Sandy Weinberg, Tim and Dabney Beck, Will and Jan Hernandez, Kathy Halowell, Michael Gabertan, Angela Jones, Annette Colón, Elaine Wilson, Nancy McDonagh, Dawnielle Materre, Becca Marie Hald, Carol Romeo, Richard and Maribel Spunt, Wallace and Charisse Bell, Laura Hubbard, Father Phil and Tamera Pelikan, John and Carol Bratun, David and Melea Brock, Bob Caron, my aunt "Cream Puff"—also known as Pat Hayes—Kathy Reese, and Lacy White. Finally, I extend sincere thanks for the prayers of my husband's Pasadena Men's Group, and those of my loving St. Andrew's MOPs mommas.

CONTENTS

FOREWORD

by Robert A. Rohm, Ph.D.

Every so often we meet someone, or we read something that influences our life for the better. These moments cannot be planned; they just happen. Some would call them a "coincidence". But those of us who are awake to the spiritual things of the Lord, call them a "God moment". We sense His presence. And even though it was unexpected, and even though we cannot see Him, we sense His nearness. After all, which one of us controls God or His timing or oversees His schedule?

In this excellent work, Maureen Broderson gives us the inside story on what is going on behind the scenes. I have often said, "I don't want to know what is going on...I want to know what is going on BEHIND what is going on!" It is one thing to watch it rain. It is another thing to know how to look at a weather app and see a storm approaching and to prepare for its arrival. The message in this book gives the reader insights to know how to deal with the darkness in this world and how to prepare to expose it to the light. We know what is going on behind the scenes thanks to people like Maureen who help show us the way.

When I became a Christian many years ago, I was basically taught that God loved me and had a wonderful plan for my life. It sounded like I was about to embark on an exciting, uplifting adventure. Eternal life was the gift of God through Jesus Christ our Lord (Romans 6:23). I was so happy! I think I had the feeling like that of getting on a *cruise ship*. Looking back, I now believe I would have been better served if I had been warned that I was entering a whole new realm. The world, the flesh and the devil are all real. I should have been told I was getting on a *battleship*! I did not understand that just because I had Jesus in my life that my daily experience would become even more fierce. Jesus warned, "In this world you will have trouble. Be of good cheer. I have overcome the world" (John 6:33). My job was to learn to walk daily with Jesus in the spirit and obey God above everything else. I just did not know how.

A person who follows the Lord wants to know His mind. After all, the main purpose for a believer in Jesus Christ should be to grow his or her faith to know the heart of God. He becomes our passion. "We are not fighting FOR victory." We are fighting from a position of victory that has already been won on our behalf by Jesus Christ. But where do you go to discover all this? How does all that work? Who can you turn to for guidance? Only someone who has been on that same journey and has personal experience can help you know the right path to follow. The answer to those questions and more is found in the book you are about to read! I only wish I could have had this information when my journey first began so many years ago.

You are about to wake up to the reality of the fact you and God make a majority. You are "more than a conqueror

through Him who loved us" and gave Himself for us
(Romans 8:37). This book can become a roadmap as you
travel through this life.

Thank you, Maureen, for the time, effort, and diligence you
put into writing this book. I love the fact you have taken
deep truths that require a lifetime to learn and offer them
in such a manner that the reader can understand them,
receive them, and put them into daily practice immediately.
That is no easy task, but you have done it!

May this book go forth with God's hand of approval, favor,
and blessing and touch many people to become better
warriors in God's Kingdom!

God bless you!

ROBERT A. ROHM, Ph.D., President
Personality Insights, Inc.
Atlanta, GA

BORN TO BE GOD'S CHAMPION

". . .overwhelming victory is ours through Christ, who loved us"

(Romans 8:37b, NLT)

You and I are created to be conquerors! Every one of us is born into a world at war with a powerful adversary. God intends that we not only challenge our enemy but victoriously overcome him. *"No, despite all these things, overwhelming victory is ours through Christ, who loved us"* (Romans 8:37, NLT).

This declaration compels the question, "What are *'all these things'*?" The answer appears throughout Scripture, and if we think about it, in our own life experience as well. "All" is everything that stands in opposition to God's plan and purpose for our lives. Sin, doubt, fear, failure, worry, weakness, hopelessness, and anything else in heaven and earth that draws us away from the love of God and the truth of His Word.

God's strategic battle plan has always been to empower and equip each one of us to live life with the confident assurance that, through Christ, we are *"more than conquerors."* "Who, me?" you ask, "You've got to be kidding!" I smile because that's what I used to think as well. I'm nobody special. I'm just a grandma. I love the Lord, I believe His Word is true, and I do my best to please Him. Still, perhaps like you, my life gets hard at times, and I don't feel anything like God's champion.

I used to accept it. That is until the day I came to understand not every difficult circumstance I face is "just the way life is." Here's the truth I've learned: the moment I became a follower of Christ, I became the adversary of a vicious enemy who wages war, seeking to devour me. It doesn't matter that I wasn't raised in Satanism or that I don't have a military background. Like it or not, I am in a war, and so are you. It is active combat with the lies of the devil and his hosts of assailants.

But don't lose heart! With God's help, it's a war we can win. The good news is we have the privilege of serving under the Commander of all of Creation. God has commissioned you and me to be aware of and vigilant against the tactics of our enemy. We are to dress in God's armor and employ the supernatural weapons of His Spirit to defeat the battle plans of the hostile spiritual forces that surround us.

Why have I written a book about spiritual warfare? Because in decades of ministry, I have met thousands of "ordinary people" who believe as I once did—that because you don't see yourself as anyone special, you think, "Why would the devil care about me?" Trust me, if you are a person of prayer, he not only knows you, he fears you— more than you might imagine.

The devil is fully aware that with God you are a mighty warrior. In Him, you have the potential to achieve extraordinary victories in the conflicts that plague your personal life, the lives of your family, your neighborhood, and the world in which we live. The wicked old serpent's only hope is that you will never find him out and decide to take God at His word to fearlessly engage the spiritual battle at hand.

Within the pages of this book, you will discover, or perhaps recapture, God's call on your life to rise and assume your rightful identity in the Spirit. The Lord of Heaven's Armies has anointed and appointed you as His agent, deployed to conquer your real enemy as Jesus Himself did. For *"the reason the Son of God appeared was to destroy the works of the devil"* (1 John 3:8b, *ESV*). Together may we, on behalf of Jesus Christ and in the miraculous power of His name, dismantle, destroy, and overcome every obstacle that would seek to hinder us from banishing the darkness in our own lives and sharing His light and love with a deeply hurting world. More than ever before, it is a message of hope the world desperately needs.

Victory can and will be yours. Read on my friend, and discover the triumphant champion God created you to be.

CHAPTER ONE

THE UNSEEN WAR IN THE SPIRITUAL REALM

"For we do not wrestle against flesh and blood, but against the rulers, against the authorities, against the cosmic powers over this present darkness, against the spiritual forces of evil in the heavenly places"

(Ephesians 6:12, *ESV*)

The days in which we live seem to grow ever darker. As I write, we are amid a global pandemic, and hundreds of thousands are sick and dying. Anxiety and fear appear inescapable. At the same time, widespread prejudice and racial injustice besiege the United States of America. The evil of radical destruction, passionate irrationality, lawlessness, anger, and violence regrettably infiltrate many protests. Politicians on both sides of the aisle lust for power and control. Our nation is by no means alone in this. We live in a world sick with anger. As anger always does, it draws our attention away from God. It overtakes His primary message of hope of transformation, justice, unity, and peace, leaving nothing but fear, heartache, and ruin in its wake.

The darkness is deceiving our children and grandchildren as it devours them with the values of a culture drifting farther and farther away from the reality of ultimate Truth. In increasing numbers, families of believers and nonbelievers in Christ are destroyed by unforgiveness, divorce, addictions, and abuse. Then, the things people escape to for relief become the very things that imprison them.

No longer can God's people neglect His call to fight. More urgently than ever before, the Church must awaken to its mission and step into the fullness of God's intention and purpose. Christ destined us to break free from Satan's enslavement, paving the way to share the love, hope, and freedom Jesus gave His life to ensure. Beloved, Jesus lived the life He intends for you and me to live! Christ modeled perfect humanity. And now He asks you to live your day-to-day life as He would live your life if He were you. Christ soundly defeated our common enemy on Calvary and now decrees that each one of us advance His triumph in every struggle we face.

The immense war raging in the spiritual realm may be invisible, but make no mistake, it is real. Scripture confirms this war is not one of setting one nation against another, nor one political party fighting against another, one race against another, and least of all people battling within their own homes and families. It is a personal battle between the flesh and the spirit, a social struggle greatly influenced by the malicious forces of darkness and a spiritual battle against evil supernatural powers. *"For we do not wrestle against flesh and blood, but against the rulers, against the authorities, against the cosmic powers over this present darkness, against the spiritual forces of evil in the heavenly places"* (Ephesians 6:12, *ESV*).

I have come to be a person who believes Jesus meant everything He said. Statements like, *"Whoever believes in Me will also do the works that I do; and greater works than these will he do..."* (John 14:12, *ESV*), and *"In My name they* (followers of Christ) *will cast out demons"* (Mark 16:17, *ESV*) are not merely suggestions; they are God's intention! It serves us well to remember one-third of Christ's earthly ministry involved confrontation with the kingdom of darkness, an action that we, His people, cannot afford to ignore. To be born into His supernatural Kingdom means that the supernatural will be natural for every person who walks out life with God.

To live in the supernatural Kingdom of God means the supernatural will be natural.

One of the greatest blessings of all is Christ did not leave us alone to fight this war. He left us *Himself* in the person of the Holy Spirit—not a percentage of the Holy Spirit, not a junior Holy Spirit. At the very moment we received Christ as our Savior and Lord, the same Holy Spirit who raised Jesus Christ from the dead became alive in us.

The immediacy of His presence equips and empowers us to live our lives, with all of our unique personal challenges, as Jesus would live them. Astonishing, isn't it?

I have answered that call, and I hope you will join me. Many times I've asked the Lord, "But who am I?" Who could imagine—a rather unremarkable woman suiting up for battle? Perhaps no one, least of all me. To look at me, I doubt anyone would view me as an adept, skillful soldier. The natural eye does not see the weapons I wield and the armor I wear. I'm simply a grandma (I must add, with three of the most handsome, brilliant grandsons ever born—grandmas get to say things like this you know).

I didn't come out of a dark, dreadful past and never entertained things having to do with witchcraft or the occult. I wasn't raised in the home of prominent Christian pastors. My parents were humble, hard-working people who taught me to honor God and do what I say I will do when I say I will do it. The most accurate description of me might be ordinary and even perhaps, mundane.

Of course, God knew all of this about me when I surrendered my life to Him over forty years ago and became a follower of Jesus Christ. Not long after, He set me on a path of learning to engage an unseen, ferocious enemy, in an invisible realm, with implications unimaginable to me.

Like my parents, my husband and I loved each other, loved our children, and raised them to the best of our ability. Having become believers in Jesus Christ shortly after our wedding day, we prayed for God's blessings to attend our family. Oh, trust me, we made plenty of mistakes along the way and often had to say, "I'm sorry." We did try our best to live a life pleasing to God. But again, to think of me as a warrior who stands against a vicious enemy? God describes me best when He said He *"has chosen the foolish things of the world to put to shame the wise, and God has chosen the weak things of the world to put to shame the things which are mighty"* (1 Corinthians 1:27, NKJ).

I had to wonder, could there be millions of "ordinary people" just like me? People doing their very best to walk out their lives completely unaware that they are in an intense spiritual battle, opposed by the hostile powers of darkness every day? And more importantly, that there is something God intends for us to do about this battle? Are we to not only fearlessly challenge but to victoriously overcome our adversary? I once heard it said, evil is powerless if the good are unafraid. Could this be so?

Gradually I began to understand the ways God intended for me to victoriously join with Him in the unseen spiritual battle and crush the hateful works of darkness. I learned that the faith-filled, expectant, and authoritative prayers of, yes, even a grandma would have a remarkable influence over my destiny and that of my children and grandchildren.

I remember Walt Disney once saying, "It's kind of fun to do the impossible!" That's exactly how I feel when I'm coming up against our adversary in the authority and power of the Lord Jesus Christ. And our God is faithful to make the seemingly impossible possible. He has chosen to partner with this ordinary grandma to extend His Kingdom in extraordinary ways. My friend, God has chosen you as well, and Satan knows it. The devil just hopes you never learned it, don't believe it, or perhaps that you've forgotten.

Let me share a story with you that clearly illustrates why this book's principles hold the promise to transform your life. A college football coach I knew was training a couple of new recruiters for the team. "Here's the deal," he began, "during the game, you're going to see a kid get knocked down, and he's not going to get back up right away. When he does, he's going to walk off the field and give up. He won't get back in the game." The recruiters-in-training inquired, "Okay, we don't want that guy, right?" "You got it," replied the coach. He continued, "Then, you'll see another kid get knocked down, get back up, and get knocked down again. He may keep getting up a few more times, but eventually, he'll give up too." "We don't want that guy either, right, Coach?" "Right. He's not the player we're looking for."

The coach went on to explain, "Then, you'll see a kid who gets knocked down over and over again, yet every time, he gets up and back in the game. He never gives up." The would-be recruiters excitedly jumped in and confidently asked, "So that's the guy we want, right, Coach?" The coach calmly said, "No, he's not the guy we're looking for either." A bit confused, our would-be recruiters then asked, "But, Coach, we don't get it. Who do we want?" After a long pause, the coach answered, "We want the guy who's knocking everybody down!"

Here's my point, God intends for you to be the one who's knocking the devil down! You don't have to put up with his assaults and malicious attempts to take you "out of the game" of your life any longer. It's time to rise in the Spirit of God and join the offensive side of this spiritual conflict.

God's plan for your victorious life of freedom is simple, but it's not always easy. So here's what to do next—commit to continue to engage this book with an open heart and the intention to discover the truth about God, the devil, and where you fit into the Lord's plans. Then, you'll learn the steps to take to become the warrior that courageously knocks Satan down in his tracks. Be assured, God will transform you! I'm confident the Lord will reveal His simple strategy and show you where the enemy has hindered you from living the abundant, overcoming life Christ gave His own life to ensure you would experience.

One question remains, "Are you ready to serve in the unseen yet genuine war as Christ's mighty soldier?" If your answer is yes, let's begin now and proclaim your commitment with me,

"Lord God, teach me to become a warrior in Your kingdom.
I welcome Your presence to protect and cover my heart, my soul, and my mind.
I declare Jesus over every family member, my home, and all You have entrusted to my care.
Come now and fill me, my family, my home, my all, with Your glory, Lord, leaving no room for anything of darkness.
In the matchless name and authority of Jesus Christ I pray, Amen."

CHAPTER TWO

IT WASN'T
THE TUNA SALAD!

A delightful expectation for tomorrow's glorious wedding day filled the room. At the rehearsal dinner, seated next to the young bride-to-be was the pastor's wife who would officiate their wedding ceremony. Over dinner, she shared a personal story of "life in ministry" with the bride-to-be, for she too was about to become a pastor's wife.

Our "seasoned" pastors were hosting a summer evening dinner party for several members of their congregation. Most of the day, the pastor's wife had lovingly prepared the meal, including a large tuna salad. It was the perfect main course on a hot, humid summer's night in Illinois. Candles reflected the soft glow of her beautifully set table, and the food looked delicious. She slipped upstairs to change.

At the sound of the doorbell, our hostess quickly came back downstairs and took one last glance into the dining room. To her horror, she saw their cat, not eyeing the tuna salad, not sniffing the tuna salad, but *in* the large, beautiful bowl of tuna salad. All four paws in the bowl! Their cat was in cat heaven.

At that moment, she had to admit, "I considered ushering our cat into literal heaven. Taking a breath to think more calmly, I lifted her out of the bowl and gently tossed her out of the back door." The doorbell rang again. "What could I do? Our guests were arriving."

She did what I probably would have done. She asked God to bless the food, scraped a thin layer off the top of the tuna salad, fluffed up the lettuce leaves, and rushed to the door to welcome their guests. "Within minutes, my husband arrived home from work, our guests had arrived, and I'd all but forgotten our cat's brazen misdeed."

The rest of the evening passed quickly. Everyone seemed to have a delightful time and loved the tuna salad, as evidenced by the empty bowl. After enjoying a wonderful evening of fellowship, the pastors bid their last dinner guests goodnight.

Tired yet content, the couple went into their kitchen to begin the task of cleaning up. Suddenly, she remembered their cat. She opened the back door to call her and once again made a startling, very unexpected discovery. On the first step of their back porch lay their cat—dead!

"Oh, dear Lord," she cried out loud! Then, a horrifying thought; the cat had eaten her tuna salad. The same tuna salad they had served. And now, their cat lay dead. Might the same fate await their guests? As embarrassing as it was, this compassionate couple quickly agreed the only right thing to do was call each of their dinner guests, humbly explain what happened, and offer to meet them at the local hospital.

Now it's essential to keep in mind this dinner-party-gone-wrong took place in the early 1960s. In those days, the accepted course of treatment in such circumstances was the rather unpleasant remedy of pumping the patient's stomach. Their dinner guests met them at the hospital, and stomach pumping is precisely what took place. As you might imagine, it was well into the early morning hours the following day before our hosts wearily returned home and climbed into bed. The dishes could wait.

Later that morning, her husband left for the church office, and she stepped back into the kitchen to finish cleaning up. There was a knock on the back door. "I opened the door and was met by our neighbor. Though he was a tall man, he stood with head bowed this particular morning and spoke in an uncharacteristically slow, sad voice. 'Ma'am, I'm sorry to tell you this, but it was so dark last night, and as I pulled into my driveway, I ran over your cat.' After a very long pause, he continued, 'And when I got to her, she was dead. I noticed a lot of cars parked in front of your house and guessed you had company. I didn't want to bother you with such bad news, so I just carefully laid your cat on the step of your back porch. I feel just terrible about it, and I'm very, very sorry.'"

She stood there, quiet, just looking at him, not knowing what to say. She thanked him for coming over and assured him of her forgiveness. Stunned, she slowly closed the door.

As I consider the dilemma these pastors found themselves in, I'm reminded of my dilemma as well. And frankly, I believe it may be one you've experienced as well.

Now this wonderful couple was the first to admit they didn't pause to pray and ask the Lord what they should do about their dead cat and their tuna-salad-consuming dinner guests. Like them, we often far too quickly come up with our own remedies to our problems, only to sadly discover they don't resolve the trouble at all. Why? Because we have wrongly determined what the actual problem is!

We try to address our fears, disappointments, anger, loneliness, or any number of life's dilemmas with worldly solutions. We decide to move away or buy a new house. Perhaps we've thought life would be better if we got a new job, or a new husband or wife, or if we just hadn't had kids. Have you ever thought, "I'll have a drink, that'll make me feel better," or "I'll go shopping," etc.? The truth is, when we wrongly diagnose our real problem, the remedies we come up with will never be adequate. More often than not, the worldly solutions we turn to produce more profound pain, conflict, and heartache. Our own remedies will never give us the freedom, contentment, or peace we long for and that God intends for us to enjoy.

So much of the believer's time is wasted, energy expended, and injury incurred because we battle people (flesh and blood) instead of the spiritual forces at work in a situation. Here's what I've learned from God's Word: the spiritual realm informs our physical realm. It's not the other way around. Unseen is not unreal, beloved! The spiritual reality is not a make-believe reality; instead, it's an entirely different reality. We have a very real enemy. An adversary busily at work to keep our eyes off the Lord and draw us away from the fulfilling intimacy of a relationship with Him. To victoriously navigate this supernatural, hope-filled reality is precisely what Jesus empowered us to live in when He *"called [us] out of the darkness into His marvelous light"* (1 Peter 2:9, *ESV*).

The spiritual realm informs our physical realm, it's not the other way around. Unseen is not unreal.

The two-fold lesson from this story is this—First, don't be afraid to enjoy a good tuna salad; it wasn't the problem. Second, let prayer be your first response to the dilemmas that arise in life. Seek God's wisdom, timing, and direction before you act on any challenges you face to discover what's really going on. *"Lord, give us Your eyes to see, Your heart to know."* Your challenge may not be with your cat or with other people for that matter. When we make war in prayer and make peace with those around us, we remove any chance the devil has of succeeding in our lives.

This is the journey I invite you to take with me as you make your way through this book. Let's do this!

CHAPTER THREE

YOU'VE GOT YOUR KEYS, RIGHT?

"And I will give you the keys of the kingdom ..."

(Matthew 16:19a)

In Old Testament times, a trumpet summoned God's people to battle. Today, a spiritual appeal sounds throughout the nations of the world. God is calling His people to arms, to be a people who will unlock the prison doors and carry His light to a world in desperate darkness. Be assured of this; the Lord's call to arms is unlike any other. It's first and foremost a call to our knees.

Let's begin with a working definition of spiritual warfare, a portion of which I learned some time ago from my pastor of nearly forty years, Dr. Jack Hayford. "Spiritual warfare engages worship and prayer—the effective outcome of which is the manifestation of the rule of God, the reign of

His power, and the revelation of His Kingdom. It is the prayerful and intentional confrontation with the demonic in the authority and power of the Holy Spirit."

God's Word clearly sets forth His plan. The Lord has commissioned His Church to act on His behalf to victoriously achieve His eternal purpose as it concerns our enemy. *"To the intent that now the manifold wisdom of God might be made known by the church to the principalities and powers in the heavenly places, according to the eternal purpose which He accomplished in Christ Jesus our Lord"* (Ephesians 3:10-11, *NKJV*). To fulfill God's purpose as responsible, Holy Spirit-empowered ambassadors of Christ is to prayerfully confront our adversary and impose God's rightful dominion throughout the earth.

In the insightful words of Paul E. Billheimer, "Prayer is not begging God to do something that He is loath to do. It is not overcoming reluctance in God. It is enforcing Christ's victory over Satan. It is implementing upon earth heaven's decisions concerning the affairs of men. Calvary legally destroyed Satan and canceled all of his claims. God placed the enforcement of Calvary's victory in the hands of the Church (*cf.* Matthew 18:18 and Luke 10:17-19) ... But this delegated authority is wholly inoperative, apart from the prayers of a believing Church."[1]

In His wisdom, God declares the Church to be His instrument to dispense on earth what He accomplished at the Cross. It is *"by the church"* that the principalities and powers in the heavenly places will know the fullness of

---

1 Paul E. Billheimer, *Destined for the Throne* (Minneapolis: Bethany House, a division of Baker Publishing Group, Nashville: Thomas Nelson Publishers, Revised edition 1996), 17.

God's eternal purpose that *"He accomplished in Christ Jesus our Lord."* Beloved, that's you and me! The ministry of Jesus Christ is now to be advanced on earth by His church. Jesus affirmed this timeless truth declaring, *"And I will give you the keys of the kingdom of heaven, and whatever you bind on earth shall be bound in heaven, and whatever you loose on earth shall be loosed in heaven"* (Matthew 16:19, *ESV*).

Oh, my friends, the keys in and of themselves are not the answer! Indeed Jesus said, *"I will give you the keys. . ."*, but merely possessing them isn't enough! My husband and I recently returned home from a brief trip to visit our daughter and family in Colorado. It wasn't until we arrived back home from the airport late at night and stood in front of our door that we discovered neither of us had our house key. As I packed to leave, I remembered thinking, "I won't need my keys in Colorado, so I'll just leave them at home." Apparently, my husband had the same thought. To leave our home safe and sound, we had diligently locked each of the doors and windows. There we stood in the dark, in front of our own home, feeling pretty silly. Inside, between us, we had at least a half dozen house keys; however, at that moment, merely owning them did us absolutely no good.

Thankfully, we hadn't left our home as secure as we initially thought. The very last window my husband checked was ajar. He was able to squeeze through this high, relatively small window and let us in. My point is this—had we had our keys in our hands, we would have utilized them to gain access and entry into the home that is rightly ours to enter.

In this same way, as children of the living God, the answer to the spiritual challenges we face each day is to take the keys He has given us in our hands. Then, employ them, understanding His Kingdom keys have functionally provided us with the right of entry, authority, and access to all of the Lord's miraculous, unlimited power. When engaged at His direction, the keys that Jesus gives release the capacity for us to victoriously engage the spiritual realm by the power of His Holy Spirit!

"God has given us the keys of the kingdom of Heaven, but He does not compel us to use them. He waits. The rest is up to us, His Church. In His triumph over Satan, He has given us the needed weapons. How well we use them is up to us."[2] God has commissioned us to employ His keys with authority, responsibility, and the integrity of Christ-like character, while always keeping our eyes focused on Him.

Jesus encountered people in their pain, and His ministry answered to the prevalent human need of bondage. In His name, He equips and empowers us to do the same. Jesus has given us both authority and the mandate to destroy the works of the devil—just as He came to earth to do (*see* 1 John 3:8).

It's important to understand that no one is exempt from the battle. All of us are engaged in this struggle, whether we like it or not and whether we acknowledge it or not. No one can view it from a distance. There simply is no neutral ground. My dad had a saying that applies here, "You're either riding on the steam roller, or you're part of the pavement."

There is no neutral ground.
You're either riding on the steam roller, or
you're part of the pavement.

---

2   Ibid., 93.

During the years I taught practical theology in seminary, I always inquired of my students on the first day of class, "Why have you enrolled in this class, and what do you want to learn?" One quarter in my spiritual warfare class, a middle-aged gentleman was the first to respond to my question. In a soft yet deliberate voice, he identified himself as a pastor and made the following comment, "I used to think that the devil was a sleeping dog that I didn't want to kick. And, I was pretty sure that if I didn't bother him, he wouldn't bother me." He continued, "But lately, some things have happened in my family and in my church that have made me realize this belief is most likely not true and holding on to it, hoping that it is, has not served me, or those I care deeply about, well. I'm at a loss. I've come here to learn everything I can about this enemy of ours and what in the world I'm supposed to do about him." Have you ever had similar thoughts?

I acknowledged his humility and transparency and shared the Scripture the Holy Spirit brought to my mind as he spoke. It is a Scripture that identified two fatal errors in his assessment of the darkness. *"Be sober-minded; be watchful. Your adversary the devil prowls around like a roaring lion, seeking someone to devour"* (1 Peter 5:8, *ESV*). First of all, the devil is most assuredly not a dog; he masquerades as a roaring lion. And secondly, he never sleeps; instead, he roams the earth seeking anyone he can devour.

Peter continues in this passage with the command to *"Resist him, firm in your faith. . ."* (vs. 9a), a declaration that calls us to stand face-to-face with our adversary and vigorously oppose him. Far too often, we easily give in to the enemy instead of resisting him. Christ is calling us to take the offensive in the power of the Holy Spirit and crush the works of darkness.

God's Word unmistakably reveals the devil is not the only one who is searching. *"For the eyes of the Lord run to and fro throughout the whole earth, to give strong support to those whose heart is blameless toward him"* (2 Chronicles 16:9, *ESV*). God's commitment to His people offers all that we need for His unique plan and purpose to come to fruition in and through our lives. He is ever searching for His own, those who call on Him amid life's struggles. And, beloved, there's only one true lion—Jesus Christ, *"the Lion of the tribe of Judah, the heir to David's throne, [who] has won the victory"* (Revelation 5:5b, *NLT*).

Know this, the enemy cannot steal your destiny. Let me say that again—the enemy cannot steal the destiny God had in His heart and mind for you before He formed you in your mother's womb. He cannot take the fullness of God's intention and purpose from you. In the words of Dr. Neil Anderson, "He can do nothing to damage your position and identity in Christ."[3] There is only one thing our adversary, the devil, can do. He can expend every effort to deceive you in the hope you will give up your intended destiny. Of this you may be assured, he is relentless in that endeavor!

The enemy cannot steal your destiny. He can only try to make you give it up.

One of my favorite Christmas carols tenderly declares, "Silent Night, Holy Night."[4] Revelation 12:12-17 sets forth the reality that the night of Christ's birth was holy, yes— yet anything but silent! Have a look with me at Revelation

---

3   Neil T. Anderson, *Victory Over the Darkness: Realizing the Power of Your Identity in Christ.* (Ventura, CA: Regal Books, 1990) 44.

4   *Silent Night.* Traditional Christmas carol by Franz Grubner. 1818, using words penned by Father Joseph Mohr.

12:17a, *ESV, "Then the dragon became furious with the woman and went off to make war on the rest of her offspring, on those who keep the commandments of God and hold to the testimony of Jesus."* Who is the darkness waging war against? Quite simply, it is every one of us who has come to the Lord in humble repentance and received Christ's forgiveness of our sins. The devil set out to make war with you and me, and he will continue to do so until Christ's glorious return.

The Bible is clear that while Christ destroyed hell's power at the cross, it is the Church's mission to extend it. Redemption was, is, and ever will be Jesus' completed work at the Cross. There is nothing we add to it, *"For by grace you have been saved through faith. And this is not your own doing; it is the gift of God, not a result of works, so that no one may boast"* (Ephesians 2:8-9, *ESV*).

Yet there remains an unfinished work of the Cross. It is the ministry of Jesus Christ. He commissioned His Church to take His Gospel message into all the world, everywhere, and to everyone (*cf.* Matthew 28:18-20)! God calls His people to be the extension of His body, and through us, His ministry continues.

Securely confident in Jesus, we don't engage this battle hoping *"for victory."* Instead, we are fighting *"from victory."* We implement Christ's rule, His reign, and His power as we advance His completed work on Calvary into our daily experience and in the lives of every person God will bring across our path. And not just on Sundays as we gather in church, but on the Mondays and Tuesdays of everyday life as well.

As the children of God, we are not fighting for victory, we are fighting from victory!

And so, the finished work of Christ is the work of redemption. The unfinished work of Christ is His ministry. The Lord's victory over Satan is the Church's victory. He now calls His followers to reach the world by the power of His life, the Holy Spirit. The Lord's strategy is to break the yokes of bondage through a people He calls His Church.

As I write, I pray that the Holy Spirit will ignite this truth in you so that what God is ready to release in heaven will be released in and through each of you who reads these words. But we can't give what we don't have. And so we begin with us. As Dr. Neil Anderson rightly asserts,

> "When you received Christ, the power of sin was not broken, but its power to dominate you was broken through your death, resurrection and righteousness in Christ (Rom. 6:7; 8:10).

> No longer do you have to sin because you are dead to sin and alive in God in Christ (Rom. 6:11). Sin still strongly appeals to your flesh to continue to act independently of God. But you are no longer bound to participate as you were before receiving Christ. It is your responsibility not to let 'sin reign in your mortal body that you should obey its lusts' (Rom. 6:12)."[5]

---

5   Ibid., Anderson, 82.

So here, now, may we, His Church, rise and welcome God's work of freedom and restoration in our lives as we continue to learn, grow, and mature in our journey to become the Church of His purpose and intention!

Lord, teach me to confidently engage the keys of Your kingdom You have given me.
Show me how to effectively fight the darkness from the powerful position of the victory You secured by Your life, death, and resurrection.
In Your name I pray, Amen.

CHAPTER FOUR

ERADICATING UNBELIEF

"So we see that they were unable to enter because of unbelief."

(Hebrews 3:19)

Have you ever heard of the television program entitled "Antique Road Show"? For those of you who may not have, the program's premise is to get some antique dealers and auction houses to team up to set up shop in local convention centers and allow people the opportunity to get free appraisals of their "stuff."

People often find out their stuff is just what they thought it was—it's stuff. But there are other times when people get a bit of a surprise. I've been told about one of those moments as it happened to a gentleman from Arizona.

The story goes, he inherited an Indian blanket from his grandmother years prior. He knew it was old, and he didn't even like it that much but kept it because of the sentimental value it had in his family. Hearing the "Antique Road Show" was in town, he thought, "What do I have to lose?"

He threw the blanket casually over his shoulder, walked out his front door, threw it into the back seat of his car, and drove to the convention hall. Indifferently, he strolled into the convention hall, waited his turn in line, then handed it to one of the appraisers.

The appraiser began to study it, then called another over. Then another gentleman joined them, and the three men began to talk with measured excitement in their voices. After spending a significant amount of time with the blanket, they faced the blanket's owner. The senior appraiser spoke in deep, deliberate tones, "Sir, your blanket appears to be one of the earliest and undoubtedly complete Navaho weavings in existence today. We can determine by the design it was created for a chief sometime during the mid-1800s. Our professional estimate is your blanket may be worth somewhere between 350 and 500 thousand dollars.

The appraisers returned his blanket as he stood speechless. Remember how he had walked in with it, uncaringly slung over his shoulder? Escorted by security, he exited the arena, his blanket now meticulously draped over both arms. He gently laid it on the back seat of his car. Cautiously he drove home, where he deposited the blanket into his safe until he could determine what to do with his newly discovered treasure.

What changed? No one miraculously transformed his blanket into something different than he came in with— same old, in his mind, rather unattractive blanket he had owned for years! What changed was his understanding of the significance and value of the blanket.

Before we move on in our study of spiritual warfare, it's critical that you not only understand but believe the significance of the role you play in the battle. Satan keeps a step ahead of you if you don't see yourself with God's eyes and come to a new place of belief in the immense value He has created within you. In the spiritual battles we currently engage in every single day, the stakes have never been higher. We must be non-negotiable in our trust in God, His Word, and sustain an unqualified belief that God's purpose for each of us in His strategic battle plan will be victoriously fulfilled, perhaps in dimensions we've never known before.

Please take a moment to stop and pray with me once again—*"I come with open heart and eyes before You, Lord, to seek and to see an enlarged perception of You. Change my understanding of, and appreciation for the significance and value You have created within me. Enlarge my faith to believe not only that Your Word is true, but also to believe the truth of all You say about me. I choose to engage life as a warrior in Your Kingdom, submitted to Your command that together we may see the plans and purposes of Satan defeated. Beginning today, give me a new perspective of the victorious life You intend for me and how to achieve it. For Your glory, Lord, these things I ask in the name of Jesus Christ, Amen."*

We begin by examining belief and unbelief. To victoriously navigate the world we live in today, thoroughly equipped to fulfill God's warrior call on our lives, we have no option but to stand firmly in the Truth. There is no room for doubt or unbelief. Society's truth seems to change every fifteen minutes. We all know things that at one time were condemned by our culture, but today are viewed as perfectly fine.

Science is always changing. Ever since I can remember, "Pluto" was a planet. Then, a while back, we were told it wasn't. Most recently, NASA informed us Pluto is a "Dwarf Planet."[6]

Think about medicine. We take a particular medication for years, and then one day, we learn it can kill us! Now don't get me wrong. Research and development in the vast fields of medicine promote change for our good to improve our lives' quality year after year. I'm not judging any of these issues as good or bad; I am just pointing out that life changes around us.

But we who hold fast to our belief in God and His Word stand firm on the One who said, "I AM" "...*the same yesterday, and today and forever*" (Hebrews 13:8, *ESV*). He does not change. The Lord is our rock and our firm foundation amid a dangerous world. In Him, "...*there is no variation or shadow of turning*" (James 1:17, *NKJV*).

Once again, I remind you, unseen is not unreal. Our physical world is a shadow of a deeper reality in the spirit. Jesus beckons us as He did Nicodemus, for from the moment we are "born again," we begin to live in

---

6   https://www.nasa.gov/audience/forstudents/5-8/features/nasa-knows/what-is-pluto-58.html

supernatural dimensions—the eternal spiritual reality of the Kingdom of God.

But unbelief will incessantly crowd in. It seeks to hold us captive in the most dangerous of ways—as prisoners unaware. We move forward to triumphantly engage spiritual warfare by first identifying and irradiating any place of unbelief within our hearts and minds.

While I don't know of anybody that can perfectly describe the time element in the redemptive workings of the Lord, this I do know—when God said, for instance, *"I AM the Lord who heals you"* (Exodus 15:26, *NKJV*), He declared an aspect of His character and His nature. The healing He refers to encompasses physical and emotional healing, freedom from pain, and deliverance from bondage. The Lord revealed Himself as the eternal, always present, always available, unchanging Lord who answers our current needs.

He said, "I AM THE LORD." Not "I will be." Not "I was" or "I hope to be one day," but "I AM." And, the Lord in revealing Himself can only describe who He is. He is eternal, utterly unlimited by time. It is the unchanging Lord who created each one of us to fulfill His intention in our lives. He *"...saved us and called us with a holy calling, not according to our works, but according to His own purpose and grace which was given to us in Christ Jesus before time began"* (2 Timothy 1:9, *NKJV*). His intention has not changed.

Whatever our present circumstances, God calls us to believe and engage His calling for our lives with our whole hearts. In years of ministry, I have observed one's unbelief can keep them from that. Remember, the author of Hebrews tells us that God's people were unable to enter into the Promised Land, not because of their grumbling or even their idol worship of the golden calf, but because of their unbelief. *"And to whom did he swear that they would not enter his rest, but to those who were disobedient? So we see that they were unable to enter because of unbelief"* (Hebrews 3:18-19, *ESV*).

When God says, "I AM," He is saying to you right now as you hold this book in your hands, "I will be with you in the present, and I will meet you in the here and now, in every battle you face. I will be with you as you navigate every detail of your life."

Even Moses did not enter into the Promised Land! God spoke to him and clearly told him why. *"...Because you did not believe in Me, to uphold Me as holy in the eyes of the people of Israel..."* (Numbers 20:12, *ESV*). Applicable to all that God does is John 8:58, *NKJV*, *"Most assuredly I say to you, before Abraham was, 'I AM.'"* The Great "I AM" is our firm foundation, and He calls us to believe.

Let's look to a familiar story to see how the heart of God responds to our unbelief, as recorded by John in the eleventh chapter of his Gospel, verses 1-44. Beginning in verse 32, we see that Mary and Martha came to Jesus weeping. They've lost their brother. What was Jesus' reaction to them? John 11:33 and 35, *ESV*, tells us that Jesus *"...was deeply moved in His spirit and greatly troubled ... [and] Jesus wept."*

The Lord compassionately wept with Mary and Martha in the pain of losing their brother. Did Jesus also grieve the loss of His beloved friend? Perhaps. However, I invite you to consider this—Scripture informs us that Jesus knew what was about to happen. He was not going to lose His friend at all. And so I have often wondered, was it their unbelief in His character, His nature, and His word that caused His heart to break?

You see, earlier in this passage, we hear Jesus say to His disciples, "...*This illness does not lead to death. It is for the glory of God, so that the Son of God may be glorified through it*" (John 11:4, *ESV*). And then Jesus goes on to tell His disciples, "...*Let us go to Judea again*" (vs. 7). The disciples, understandably worried about His safety, objected, but Jesus went on to patiently explain, "*Our friend Lazarus has fallen asleep, but I go to awaken him*" (vs. 11). Still, they argued, seemingly clueless of what was going on, "*Lord, if he has fallen asleep, he will recover*" (v. 12b). And so Jesus made it clear, "*Lazarus has died, and for your sake I am glad that I was not there so that you may believe. But let us go to him*" (*cf.* vs. 14-15).

Mary, Martha, and those with them believed Jesus had failed them. I suggest for you to believe He is unfaithful, or He hasn't heard you cry out to Him, or He has failed you, is like saying, "You are not who You said You are!" Scripture tells us we trouble the heart of God when we don't trust Him and believe Him, and He weeps.

God's ways are not ours, and His timing is nothing like ours. He created time, and therefore most assuredly lives outside of time. Yet, despite my faith, there have been times I've allowed myself to give place to unbelief when I didn't see the Lord respond to me in the way I wanted Him to or at the time I thought He should. Have you ever been there? Such a response compels us to ask ourselves,

"Are we living for God's glory or our comfort and convenience?"

Pastor and author Mark Batterson observes, "I can almost guarantee that our hopes and dreams will take longer than our original estimates. But here's the point: we give up too easily, too quickly. We often get ahead of God, instead of keeping in step with His Spirit or we fall behind out of frustration."[7] God alone knows the timing. He moves at the time when it will bring the most glory to Him. Once again, He calls us to trust and believe.

Getting back to Mary and Martha's encounter with their unbelief, consider John 11: 39-40. We interestingly see that Jesus asked them to roll the gravestone away. Have you ever wondered, "Those gravestones are huge and very heavy! Couldn't He have done it?" Jesus created that immense stone! Yet He said, *"Did I not tell you that if you believed you would see the glory of God?"* and He required those who had gathered to roll it away. Could that gravestone have been a representation of a stone of unbelief that covered their hearts? A stone they needed to move away physically?

Even a pebble of unbelief can block God's power in and through our lives, just as it did in the lives of the people in Jesus' hometown of Nazareth. Scripture records that there *"He could do no mighty work ... And He marveled because of their unbelief"* (*cf.* Mark 6:1-6). Christ longs to free us from the darkness of unbelief. He calls us to believe and become partakers of our heavenly calling by inviting us to

---

7   Mark Batterson, *Whisper: How to Hear the Voice of God* (New York: Multnomah, 2018),152.

participate with Him in the miraculous, supernatural realm of His Kingdom.

Unbelief will block the power of God in and through our lives.

Once again, the author of the letter to the Hebrews warns us, *"Beware, brethren, lest there be in any of you an evil heart of unbelief in departing from the living God"* (Hebrews 3:12, *ESV*). Departing from the living God is an abandonment of our faith. It's turning away from God and turning away from the Word of God incarnate, His Son Jesus Christ (*cf.* John 1:1,14). Such a posture is most assuredly the design and purpose of the adversary himself, to keep us from fulfilling all that God has intended for us. Beloved, we have both the ability and responsibility to keep God present in our minds and choose to believe! The late, brilliant theologian, Dr. Dallas Willard, taught me, "The ultimate freedom we have as individuals is the power to select what we will allow or require our minds to dwell upon and think about."[8]

The focus of your thoughts significantly affects everything else that happens in your life. Your thoughts evoke the feelings and beliefs that frame your world and motivate your actions. Ultimately, what you believe rules you. If you think your life's purpose is simply to fill limited roles, you'll fill them and stop there—never knowing more was available to you. Jesus asserts that it's natural for His people to partner with Him in the supernatural world we have been born into and believe for the miraculous.

---

8   Dallas Willard, *Life Without Lack: Living in the Fullness of Psalm 23* (Nashville: Thomas Nelson, 2018), 3.

Consider with me the words of Elizabeth to Mary, the mother of Jesus, *"You are blessed because you believed that the Lord would do what He said"* (Luke 1:45, *NLT*). Mary entered into the promise of God because of her unqualified belief in Him and His Word. How deeply thankful I am.

Think about the faith of the Roman centurion. *"Then Jesus said to the centurion, 'Go your way; and as you have believed, so let it be done for you.' And his servant was healed that same hour"* (Matthew 8:13, *NKJV*). What he believed could happen did happen!

In these few Scriptures, we see the consequence of both our belief in God's Word and our unbelief. I've found that some people tend to think of consequences negatively, a punishment perhaps. The truth is there are consequences to everything we do.

Simply defined, consequence is the effect, result, or outcome of something occurring earlier. Please make no mistake; we will experience the consequences of every thought and action, either for our good or our harm, our gain or our loss. The choice is always ours.

To fully understand what God calls us to believe about ourselves, we must return to the garden and begin at the beginning. Here we see the truth that our story does not begin with sin; it begins with glory bestowed upon you by God. It does not start with Genesis, Chapter Three. Our story begins with Genesis, Chapter One. *"So God created man in His own image, in the image of God He created him; male and female He created them"* (Genesis 1:27, *ESV*).

And the Psalmist penned, *"When I look at the night sky and see the work of your fingers—the moon and the stars you have set in place—what are mortals that you should think of us, mere humans that you should care for us? For you made us only a little lower than God, and you crowned us with glory and honor"* (Psalm 8:3-5, *NLT*).

The Lord, our God, is glorious beyond measure. You and I are His children, His reflection, His likeness, and we bear His image. He made the heavens and the earth in all their glory and said, "It was good" (Genesis 1:25b, *ESV*). Only after He created man did He say, *"It was very good"* (Genesis 1:31, *ESV*).

Think of it! God endowed you and me with glory so deep that all creation pales in comparison. It is a glory unique to each of us, just as our fingerprints are unique to us. A glory our hearts long to rediscover.

Let's quickly explore the biblical perspective of glory. The Hebrew word, *kavod*, translated "glory," literally means "heavy or weighty, and is linked to the concept of authority and respect. It's an understanding that appears today when we refer to someone who "carries a lot of weight," importance and dignity.[9]

In reference to humankind, Adam and Eve represented God with full authority. Interestingly, "the Greek word for 'glory,' *Doxa,* involves the concept of recognition. More precisely, it is that which causes something or someone to be recognized for what it really is."[10]

---

9   https//: en.wikipedia.org/ wiki/ Glory_(religion).

10 Zodhiates, *Hebrew-Greek Key Study Bible*, p. 1826.

When we read in Scripture, humankind is God's glory (*cf.* 1 Corinthians 11:7), it is telling us God is to be recognized in humans. Why? So humans can accurately represent Him. I invite you to pause a moment and think about the parts of the word itself "re" and "present." Therein, God commissions us to ongoingly present His glory in the Earth and the heavenly realms.

When creation looked at Adam and Eve, they were supposed to see God. And they did! That is until Adam and Eve disobeyed and fell short of His glory. No longer was God recognized in fallen humankind. For this recognition to be realized once again and regain the privilege and responsibility to represent Him, He sent His Son. Washed in the cleansing blood of Jesus Christ, we are transformed back into God's image once again, *"from glory to glory"* (2 Corinthians 3:18, *NKJV*).

Just as our story didn't begin with sin, it does not end with sin! It ends with glory restored! In his letter to the Romans, the Apostle Paul declares, *"...those whom He justified He also glorified"* (Romans 8:30b, *ESV*). The enemy would like nothing better than to have us believe otherwise. He deceives us and tries to cover us with a veil in an attempt to hinder us from living from our glory.

But wait! Have a look with me at 2 Corinthians 3:16-18 as penned in the New Living Translation, *"But whenever someone turns to the Lord, the veil is taken away. Now the Lord is the Spirit, and where the Spirit of the Lord is, there is freedom. And we, who with unveiled faces all reflect the Lord's glory, are being transformed into his likeness with ever-increasing glory, which comes from the Lord, who is the Spirit."*

Therefore, having turned to the Lord, we will, with unveiled face, bring freedom, transformation, a new heart, and His likeness to every situation we face in life. All of which will be attended by His glory.

Pride often lingers about here, looking for an open door. Accordingly, we must be confident in our understanding that we only reflect the image of something we stand directly in front of. God calls us to look directly into the face of our precious Savior. He is beckoning us to stand so close to Him that others will see only Christ's reflection in us. And then, in true humility, our lives will bring honor to Him.

If we think for even a moment that we are the source of the power of God, we are most sadly mistaken. It is the Holy Spirit and Him alone who comes in power. Without an intimate relationship with the fullness of the Godhead, we are bankrupt, impoverished indeed.

There's a balance here because God does not call you to ignore His design and creative intention. He calls you to believe He created you to bear His glory and become a reflection of Him. Picture yourself faithfully standing before Him, totally dependent upon Him. In those moments, He extends the invitation and privilege to you to partner with Him in piercing the darkness with His light, thus advancing His kingdom.

You may be asking, "Why does any of this matter?" Why is there an entire chapter addressing unbelief in a book about spiritual warfare? The answer is quite simple. Beloved, you can't give what you don't have. Empowerment and equipping for warfare begins with you and then reaches beyond.

Read Jesus' own words as recorded in John 7:38, *NLT*, *"Anyone who believes in Me may come and drink! For the Scriptures declare, 'Rivers of living water will flow from his heart.'"* Living water, rivers of it, the life of the Holy Spirit will flow from your heart into your own life and into the lives of those you encounter each day.

At times, we think so small! We think about our stories and mistakenly believe that's all life is. But God invites us to the adventure of participating in His grand story. Each of us has a role to play, and we've got to show up, believing God is who He says He is and that He will do what He says He will do. In and through us, He will destroy the works of the devil.

Let me conclude this chapter with a brief, personal story. When I was a young girl, my brother taught me an effective strategy to assemble a puzzle. Here's what he said, "First, you find the corner pieces. These are the most significant pieces of the puzzle. Find them and set them in place. Then, find the edge pieces, those with a straight side. These pieces are next in order of significance. Ranking third in significance are the pieces that you can group by similar colors or recognizable objects. Lastly, you'll need to figure out what to do with the insignificant pieces, the non-descript pieces. Simply fill them in as you're able."

Stepping into adulthood, I realized that I had adopted this "puzzle strategy" to judge or "rank" people ... especially myself! I had "corner piece people" in my life, people I considered to be extraordinarily significant and more important than I could ever hope to be. Highly favored people, more gifted, talented, better looking, and much more influential than I was. The people I believed God had uniquely gifted and used in remarkable ways—ways the Lord would never consider using me. You get the picture.

I also had friends who seemed to be "wonder woman moms." Looking back now, I'm confident it wasn't true. Still, at the time, I determined they had perfect marriages, were raising perfect kids and lived in perfect homes as they enjoyed successful, professional careers. I compared myself to them. I judged myself, concluding that I was one of the "last to be chosen, insignificant" pieces in the puzzle of life. Because of choices I'd made and challenging events in my life, I saw myself as a nondescript puzzle piece with bumps and bruises.

Years later, one Christmas, as we do from time to time, our family was enjoying putting a puzzle together. I remembered the strategy I had learned long before and decisively implemented it. But let me ask you something, have you ever put a puzzle together only to come to the end to discover a missing piece? Oh man, incredibly disheartening, isn't it? After days of working on our puzzle, that's what happened to us.

Amid the disappointment, God whispered a question to my heart, "Which piece has now become the most significant piece of the puzzle?" I think you know the answer—the missing piece! Suddenly, this seemingly insignificant, nondescript piece had become the essential piece, for without it, the picture was incomplete.

At that moment, God affirmed He had uniquely created me, with intention and purpose, to fulfill a unique role in His story. I needed to step up to the plate and execute it.

I became aware for the first time, if I continued to "not show up" in life, I was no different than that missing piece. The picture of God's design would be incomplete. I had stepped back from all God had created me to be for far too long.

I realized if I continued in this ungodly belief, I would never experience all the Lord intended me to be or carry out all He created me to do. After so many years of not believing God had a plan and purpose for me, at last, I understood no matter what shape I am, or what dents and bumps life's journey and the choices I'd made have given me, it did not change the reality I am significant and deeply valued by God. I've seen God use the lessons learned from my life experiences, good and bad, as the very weapons He employs to overcome the schemes of Satan himself.

In God's eyes, our past mistakes for which He forgives us never invalidate His purposes for our present and our futures. We each have a unique role to play. It doesn't matter if the Lord sets us into the story He's writing as the first piece or the very last piece. What matters is that we show up when God asks us to, and we do so with excellence. In those moments, His story will be complete, and His intention fulfilled.

In God's eyes, our past mistakes for which He forgives us never invalidate His purposes for our present and our futures.

My friend, I encourage you to believe you are significant. Believe you are deeply loved. Believe you have tremendous value and a decisive role to play in the natural and the spiritual realms. As God declared to Jeremiah long ago, He declares to you today, *"Before I formed you in the womb I knew you. Before you were born I sanctified you; I ordained you . . ."* (Jeremiah 1:5a, *NKJV*).

One more thing—attending this understanding is a great responsibility; to be the most extraordinary piece of the puzzle you're to be. For without you, the story God is writing will be incomplete and never fully brought to fruition as He gloriously intends.

It's important to stop comparing yourself to others. Their "piece of the puzzle" is different from yours. Not better or worse, not more or less crucial, just different. God will guide, equip and empower you to be the unique person He created you to be. Step into your calling and silence the lies of darkness that continue to draw you into unbelief. God will help you become all He intends for you to be. However, be assured He will never help you be someone else.

God is calling you to trust and believe you're significant, deeply loved, and you have tremendous value and great responsibility in the Kingdom of God. The Lord affirmed this truth in the first letter of Peter, *". . .for you are a chosen people. You are royal priests, a holy nation, God's very own possession. As a result, you can show others the goodness of God, for he called you out of the darkness into his wonderful light"* (1Peter 2:9, *NLT*).

While God alone is responsible for your life and ministry's outcome, the choices you make will have a significant impact. God has determined not to override your will. As a follower of Christ, your inescapable responsibility is to listen for His voice and obediently respond to what He calls you to do, say, or at times, what not to say and pray.

God is calling you to trust and believe.

Will you once again bow your heart with me in prayer?
"Lord, as You asked of Jairus when You went to heal
his daughter (see Luke 8:40-50),
You ask of me today that I would never fear Your plan
and purpose for my life;
but rather simply believe (cf. Luke 8:50).
Help me not be like the people in Your hometown
of Nazareth, robbed of the miraculous move of God
because of their unbelief (see Mark 6:3-6).
Forgive me for my unbelief, Lord.
From this moment forward, I choose to engage life with
the confidence of being Your representative. Help me,
Jesus, to accurately reflect Your glory and live into the
power and authority You have given me, always in
obedient response to Your voice.
Let me fearlessly advance Your kingdom on Earth as it
is in heaven and overcome the darkness, in Your name.
Today, Lord, I choose to believe You and live into all
that You have created Your Church and me to be and
to do, 'to the intent that now the manifold wisdom
of God might be made known by the church to the
principalities and powers in the heavenly places'
(Ephesians 3:10, NKJV). Amen."

Moving ahead, have you ever wondered, does God still speak today? And, if so, will He speak to me? Read on my friend, for in the next chapter, you'll discover the answer to these two questions.

CHAPTER FIVE

HEARING GOD'S VOICE

---

*"My sheep hear My voice, and I know them,
and they follow Me."*

(John 10:27, *ESV*)

Every entity engaged in battle in the spiritual realm "sees" what's going on; everyone except us, that is! God sees and knows. The angels see the dynamics of each assault. Our adversary, the devil, sees, as do his host of demons. Everyone sees but us. Simply, yet most profoundly stated, we must hear the voice of the living God for revelation, direction, timing, and guidance if we hope to be victoriously effective in the unseen spiritual conflict. Without God's voice to guide us in the unseen supernatural realm, we are left spiritually disadvantaged— impoverished, to say the least.

On another note, not all of our problems come from Satan. If you're like me, you have most likely experienced you're more than capable of making trouble for yourself without any help from the adversary. Unfortunately, we cannot "cast out" flesh. Oh, how I wish we could! Life would be so much easier. To experience victory over oneself, you gain knowledge about your unprofitable human habits and discipline your flesh. It won't ever happen by hoping or by trying; it will only happen by training.

On the other hand, you cannot discipline or counsel a demon. You can't manage the darkness, nor can you life coach evil into leaving you alone. Following the example Jesus set for us as He navigated life on earth, you cast demons out in the power and authority God has given to all who live in His Kingdom. We'll be taking an in-depth look at power and authority in the next chapter.

The simple truth is you can't cast out flesh and you can't life coach or counsel a demon.

When our adversary engages us in battle, his strategies can be most effective. God calls us to be alert, and Peter reminds us to *"Be sober-minded; be watchful. Your adversary the devil prowls around like a roaring lion, seeking someone to devour. Resist him, firm in your faith..."* (1 Peter 5:8,9a, ESV). "To watch," as used in this passage, speaks of keeping awake or spiritual alertness. The word is intensely instructive to us, cautioning us to never be off our guard and ever mindful that our enemy will never be off of his. Think back with me to the prophet Habakkuk. He inquired of God and then said, *"I will take my stand at my watchpost and station myself on the tower and look out to see what He will say to me..."* (Habakkuk 2:1a, ESV). Habakkuk was determined to stand as a sentry posted to protect an ancient city from a surprise attack. He was ever watchful for the slightest movement. The prophet resolved to remain vigilant, that he would not miss even the smallest sign God was about to speak.

So must we, for to rise and assume our role in the Spirit as a watchman is to be unceasingly alert to the unexpected. An attack could come at any time and from any direction, and it very well could be camouflaged or disguised. Again, we recognize it is utterly impossible to effectively engage in this unseen war without God's voice to guide us. To hear God's voice is one of the highest privileges anyone could ever hope to experience. To engage God's voice is to tap into His infinite knowledge, His immeasurable goodness, and His inestimable power.

To engage God's voice is to tap into His infinite knowledge, His immeasurable goodness, and His inestimable power.

"Whoever has ears to hear, let them hear." Six times in the Gospels and eight times in the book of Revelation, Jesus repeats these eight words. Pastor and author Mark Batterson asserts, "It's the simplest of statements, but the implications are exponential. The exhortation is urgent."[11] The bottom line, God would not advise us to listen for His voice and to hear Him if it was not His intention to speak to us.

One of the enemy's strategies is to bombard our minds and thoughts with lies, confusion, fears, and doubts, at times causing us to hold God at arm's length.

---

11 Ibid., Batterson, 41.

Subsequently, we often miss His voice, thereby His wisdom and His leading. We then engage in life and the relentless spiritual conflict around us, unaware of His guidance and His revelation. It is to enter into the battle without the sword the Lord provides for us. "...*And, take the helmet of salvation, and the sword of the Spirit, which is the word of God...*" (Ephesians 6:17, ESV).

In responding to Pilate's inquisition before being delivered to be crucified, Jesus revealed, *"Everyone who is of the truth listens to my voice"* (John 18:37b, ESV). Hearing and listening to the voice of God, how do we do that? Let me share a personal example that helped me understand how to sharpen my hearing and recognize the voice of God. I have a close friend who held a distinguished rank in the Navy and a high-security clearance. One evening we were talking about the ability to discern between truth and error. He explained to me when he studied to recognize counterfeit money, he was given genuine cash and told to familiarize himself with it. The instruction was to learn every detail of the genuine article. That way, when presented with a counterfeit bill, he would be quick to recognize it. The same is true with hearing the voice of God.

But how can we be sure that it is God's voice we hear and not the enemy's, or the unrelenting voice of our fleshly desires? By familiarizing ourselves with what He has already said in His Word, the Bible. In doing so, we will come to recognize His voice. It's important to understand, when God speaks to us today, whether audibly or inaudibly, He will only say things that are in agreement and aligned with His Word.

We can learn to recognize God's voice like the prophet Samuel did when he was a young boy. He heard God call his name but didn't realize it until Eli, the chief priest, instructed him. Eli was a man familiar with God's voice, for he repeatedly heard, listened to, and responded to that voice many times throughout his life (*see* 1 Samuel 3:1-10).

As noted in the sub-title of this chapter, Jesus said, *"My sheep hear my voice, and I know them, and they follow Me"* (John 10:27, *ESV*). As followers of Jesus Christ, our primary antidote to the counterfeits the world holds out to us is knowing and recognizing God's voice, a sensitivity we will only learn and develop by spending time with Him daily.

Consider with me the television reception you may have in your home. Your preferred network is broadcasting right now. As you sit reading this book, do you hear it right now? Unless your television is currently on as you read, you don't. Now, you can be sad and complain about it, lamenting your favorite network must not care about you anymore. Or, you can take responsibility to go into the room where your television is, verify its power source, turn your TV on, and dial in. In the moments of silence, the network was doing its part. They weren't ignoring you; they were broadcasting. But again, it is your responsibility to take the initiative to position yourself to receive the signal. It's the same with hearing the voice of God. You have to position yourself to listen to His voice, and you do that by spending quality time daily in prayer, in His Word, and in silent communion with an expectation of His presence.

One of my workplace experiences clearly illustrated this truth for me. After completing an intensive course of study and being employed for over a decade as a paralegal in a sole practitioner's office, I interviewed for a new position in a much larger firm. I was thrilled to be hired to assume the roles of senior litigation paralegal and office manager.

On my first day of work, the senior partner handed me several dictation tapes and asked me to transcribe them exactly as he had spoken them. I know, cassette tapes, I'm revealing my age here. As you can tell, this was many years ago. What I quickly discovered was he was good at dictation! He left nothing to interpretation, noting not only the words but also each punctuation mark. I thought to myself, "Well, this will be a good way to get to know my new employer and learn what his expectations are." This practice continued as weeks turned into months. I became discontented, for it seemed to me he could have hired anyone who simply knew how to type to engage such a mundane, relatively boring task. Dull was not the word I envisioned to describe my new job.

Respectfully, I requested a meeting with the attorney and humbly inquired, "Why did you hire me and pay me a generous salary to merely transcribe dictation tapes, when my education and experience have equipped me to do so much more for you?" He answered simply, "This is the way I train the people I will come to expect the most out of and will chiefly rely on in the future." "How long do you anticipate this training will continue?" I asked. His ambiguous response, "Until I believe I can trust that you have learned to think as I think."

Several more months passed, when one day, I was, at last, asked to draft several letters. I was excited, to say the least! Within a short time, the attorney entrusted me with the work I enjoyed and challenged me the most: legal research and drafting pleadings. During those months of preparation, I had come to know how my attorney would respond to commonly asked questions and situations, for I had now heard him repeatedly speak to the issues. I became familiar with his viewpoint, his wording, and his style. I had come to "know his voice." Over time I excelled in that position and worked there for many years before pursuing my seminary education.

In much the same way, as you spend intimate, extended time with God and His Word, it becomes ongoingly easier to discern His voice readily. When you deal with God's Word, you deal with God Himself! God's heart and His ways will become familiar to you. He will transform your thoughts and renew your mind to align with His heart and mind (*see* Romans 12:2). You will readily recognize the Lord's revelation, wisdom, and timing, all of which are critical elements of victorious spiritual warfare. As author Maria Goff has concluded, "God wants us to know what He has to say. We won't know what He has to say about what He wants if we don't read what He said. The Bible is His voice on paper."[12]

When you deal with God's Word, you deal with God Himself.

God speaks to us primarily through the Bible, but, at times, we also hear God's voice in our consciences, our circumstances, and through other people. By inquiring of

---

12 Maria Goff, *Love Lives Here*. (Nashville: B&H Publishing Group, 2017). 160.

God's Spirit and filtering what we see and hear through the Scripture, the Lord has assured us we will truly hear His voice.

When listening for God's direction, we can't assume it will always be with an audible voice. He speaks to our spirits, and we may experience a sense of peace or unrest in our hearts. In Paul's letter to the Colossian church, he wrote, *"...let the peace that comes from Christ rule in your hearts"* (Colossians 3:15a, *NLT*). In this verse, *peace* means to be without trouble or worry, and if His peace rules in our hearts, might we allow it to be the decision-maker? When faced with a decision, if God says, "yes," we may sense His peace in our hearts or a gentle nudge. If He's saying "no," there may be unrest in our hearts. Again, inquire of the Lord, our Shepherd, who *"guides [us] along right paths, bringing honor to His name"* (Psalm 23:3b, *NLT*).

Let's think about pain for a moment; might God ever speak to us through pain? On a personal level, could pain be a way that He would reveal an area in your life in which He longs to set you free? In my experience, the presence of God amid difficult days is as real as anything I've ever felt. I ask you to consider with me, "Just because something isn't in the Bible doesn't make it unbiblical. By unbiblical, I mean contrary to the teaching of Scripture ... as long as the methodology doesn't contradict orthodox theology, we're on good ground. We might even be on holy ground."[13]

Here's what I've discovered: pain can be a theology professor; pain can be a marriage counselor; pain can be a life coach. Have you noticed nothing seems to get

---

13 Ibid., Batterson, 40.

our full attention quite like pain does? It breaks down false idols and false motives and reveals where we need to heal, where we need to grow. It exposes places that God longs for us to see the enemy defeated. Pain can be a "north star," leading us to the path of freedom from bondage. Believing this, my prayer for you won't be that you will live a pain-free life; instead, you will learn to discern God's loving voice and His tender embrace in the midst of your pain.

We will also hear God's voice by His Spirit through His revelation gifts: the Word of Knowledge, Word of Wisdom, and Discerning of Spirits. He speaks through His utterance gifts: those of prophecy, tongues, and interpretation of tongues (*cf.* 1 Corinthians 12:1-11). In his book *No Small Snakes: A Journey Into Spiritual Warfare,* Gordon Dalbey asserts, "The gifts of the Holy Spirit reveal the spiritual reality that we cannot see with our natural human perception—and thereby alert us to the enemy's presence and intent."[14] And so we understand that to face the spiritual battle at hand and to prepare to win it, we must be very intentional to listen for the voice of God, in the various ways He chooses to speak to His people, with a heart that is willing to obey.

To be effective spiritual warriors, we must realize three voices speak to us throughout each day. At any given moment, we will hear either the voice of God, our voice (the voice of our flesh), or the voice of darkness. It is utterly impossible to respond rightly unless we know who is speaking to us!

---

14 Gordon Dalbey, *No Small Snakes, A Journey Into Spiritual Warfare.* (Nashville: Thomas Nelson, 2008), 127.

Unless you know who is speaking to you, you cannot hope to respond rightly.

Here's the moment compelling us to utilize the spiritual gift of Discerning of Spirits, which God described through the Apostle Paul as *"...the ability to distinguish between spirits..."* (1Corinthians 12:10b, *ESV*). We must inquire of the Spirit of Truth, the Holy Spirit, who leads us into all Truth. Once again, Paul instructs us, *"But test everything that is said. Hold on to what is good"* (1 Thessalonians 5:21, *NLT*). We responsibly test what we hear by Scripture and determine whether it aligns with the truth of God's Word or contrary to it. Then, we respond in obedience to the voice of God. To the cries of our flesh, we respond with discipline. And when the enemy speaks, we *"resist the devil, and he will flee from you"* (James 4:7, *ESV*).

Many years ago, Jerry Dirmann, the Senior Pastor of The Rock in Anaheim, California, taught me, "One of the greatest risks of ministry is that it can be learned." We must make room for and welcome God's voice; in case He's got something in mind that, perhaps, we didn't expect! Suppose we "learn" to "do ministry," especially that of spiritual warfare, by merely thinking we can develop and follow a list of formulas instead of listening for and responding to the voice of the living God. In that case, the action of His Spirit and His power will not attend our efforts. Without the Lord's leading, we will be miserably ineffective.

I was sitting in a local coffee shop one afternoon, grading papers, before teaching a seminary class on spiritual warfare. That particular evening the topic to be addressed was this one, hearing God's voice and obediently following His direction. As I worked, it began to rain. Within minutes, it was raining so hard I could barely see my car parked right outside the window in front of which I sat. The pounding rain continued, and I became concerned for my students' safety as they drove in to attend class. I prayed and asked the Lord to please cause the rain to stop. Instantly I heard the sound of His voice in my heart, saying, "In My name, you command the rain to stop."

The forthrightness of God's directive took me by surprise. In the moments that followed, I recalled the event recorded by Matthew in Chapter 14 of his Gospel, when Jesus fed the 5,000 (plus women and children!) In essence, the disciples said, "Send the crowd away so they can go to the village and buy food for themselves." Jesus responded, "That isn't necessary; you feed them." With that statement, Jesus invited His disciples to participate in a miracle, and that's the same invitation He issued to me that day; "You command the rain to stop." And so I did. I didn't stand up or shout. I simply whispered in obedient faith, "In the name of Jesus, I command this rain to stop."

I'm embarrassed to admit my utter amazement, but immediately the rain ceased! It happened so abruptly, some of the people in the coffee shop stood up, went to the windows, and stared outside, marveling at what had just taken place.

I assure you, there simply is not a formula or "checklist" prayer I could have prayed that would have culminated in all God had in His heart and mind to teach me that day. It was a dramatic lesson of listening to and obeying God's voice, one that just an hour or so later, I would share with the students in my spiritual warfare class. I was in awe of God to have given me this remarkably clear example of the truth entrusted to me to present.

We are all called to listen for and recognize God's voice and then, without doubt, obediently respond. When we do, the Lord affords us the extraordinary privilege of partnering with God to advance His Kingdom and demonstrate His glory to the realm of darkness.

Perhaps, you may still be wondering how hearing God's voice relates to obedience, engaging spiritual warfare, and living in the freedom Christ gave His life to provide us. Let's look to King David for the answer to each element of this query: *"How can a young person stay pure? By obeying your word ... I have hidden your word in my heart, that I might not sin against you"* (Psalm 119:9,11, *NLT*). Applying King David's counsel to the warfare tactic Jesus modeled for us as He engaged Satan in the wilderness (*cf.* Matthew 4:1-11 and Luke 4:1-13), we understand that to be most effective in battle, we must confront the wiles of darkness with God's Word. But how can we if we don't know His Word? Regretfully, many of us have held our Bibles in our hands, yet we've neglected to hide God's words in our hearts.

We've held our Bibles in our hands, yet we've neglected to hide God's words in our hearts.

In the heated moments of temptation and battle, it will never be timely to Google God's Word in search of an applicable Scripture. Scripture doesn't instruct us to hide it in our cell phones. We must read, study, and commit God's Word to memory, thus hiding it in our hearts.

The reality is when we disobey, we give an opportunity to the enemy. To sin is to invite Satan's influence in our lives, opening the door to all that is at enmity with God. This compels the question, how can we obey something we're not even aware of? We can't. Therefore, it is vital that we attentively listen for God's voice. We need to know His Word and hide it in our hearts so that we will be able to, without hesitation, apply it in our engagement in spiritual warfare, culminating in the life of freedom Christ gave His life to provide for us.

This truth became astonishingly clear to me many years ago as I began to learn to minister God's freedom to people influenced by the darkness. I was sitting in church during a mid-week evening service, listening intently as our pastor proclaimed the Word of God. A lovely, middle-aged woman, whom I'd never met before, was seated next to me. She entered into worship as the service began and appeared to be engaged in the teaching.

As the service continued, I noticed she became uncomfortable, even agitated. I turned and whispered to her, "Are you all right?" She bowed her head and closed her eyes. Moments later, she looked up and turned to me. In a low, gravelly voice, a voice not her own but one of evil, spoke these words, "She will never be free of me. I have been in this family for generations. And, don't think you can tell me to leave either—you don't even know my name."

To say I was caught off guard and a bit frightened would be an understatement. Yet, all of a sudden, I found myself

leaning in and calmly, quietly yet authoritatively, spoke
these words in her ear, "*I don't need to know your name, for
I know '...the name that is above every name, so that at the name
of Jesus every knee should bow, in heaven and on earth and under
the earth...*" (Philippians 2:9b-10, ESV). *And, it doesn't matter
how long you have been in this precious woman's family, for Jesus
has declared, 'Truly, truly, I say to you, before Abraham was,
I AM'* (John 8: 58, ESV). *And so, in the matchless name of Jesus
Christ, I command you to be still and to leave this woman now.*"

Once again, the woman slowly closed her eyes, bowed
her head, and breathed out a very long, deep breath. She
sat perfectly still, her eyes remaining closed. After several
minutes, which honestly seemed like an hour to me,
slowly, she raised her head and opened her eyes. Tears
began to fall from her eyes as she whispered to me, "Did
I fall asleep? I don't know what's just happened, but it's
like I feel God's presence embracing me. For the first time
in many years, I feel at peace." I didn't sense the need
to explain; I hugged her instead and simply whispered,
"Thank you, Lord."

Without even disrupting the service, Jesus Christ set this
woman free. All I did was obediently speak His Word.
Without hesitation, He brought to my remembrance that
which I had committed to Him, the Word of God that I had
memorized years before, and He gave me the instruction
and confidence to speak it (*see* John 14:26). I didn't pause
to ask myself, "What can I possibly say or do right now?"

At that moment, I heard myself immediately proclaim
His Word. It was almost as if I was an observer, listening
to myself speak. I remember thinking, "Oh wow, Lord,

what a perfect response!" At times, I do have to laugh at myself. And who could have imagined this grandma, sitting in the pew on a Wednesday evening, had just become a warrior in God's army? I had been given the extraordinary privilege to partner with the Lord in battle as He brought a woman out from the prison where she had sat in darkness for so long (*see* Isaiah 42:7). I have no doubt it would not have happened in the way it did had I not hidden God's Word in my heart.

And so to my point, I had committed these Scriptures to heart. In those moments, I didn't have the opportunity to look for relevant verses in my concordance. This encounter took place in the years before I had access to Google in the palm of my hand. I know, can you imagine? Again, I'm telling you my age, but you get my point. I will never forget this confrontation with the darkness, the faithfulness of God to this precious woman, and His faithfulness to me as well.

In the days that followed, I pondered the engagement I'd had with the enemy that evening in church. I inquired of the Holy Spirit, asking Him to reveal the lessons I was to learn from this experience. There were several. First, as God said to Isaiah, He says to each of us today, *"I have put My words in your mouth. . ."* (Isaiah: 51:16, *NKJV*). He will faithfully give us His words to speak as we minister and serve Him.

As He has promised, God will put His words in our mouths.

I also learned that demons aren't deaf! On this particular evening in the stillness of a church service, I did not have to shout as I confronted the darkness. God instructed me to whisper His words quietly. There was no disruption of the service. I doubt that anyone around us was even aware of the battle between good and evil taking place in those moments.

From time to time, my experience that evening occurred in Jesus' ministry as well; a demon will manifest to taunt or intimidate. Most often, however, they do not. It's more common that they leave in the same way they enter, with a breath, a person being mostly unaware. I learned there are times when God will reveal the name or characteristics of the darkness so there can be repentance and an intentional commitment to refuse further association with the particular sinful behavior. In contrast, at other times, like this one, God will choose to do a sovereign work beyond our understanding.

Here's what I know, *"Therefore, if the Son makes you free, you shall be free indeed"* (John 8:36, NKJV). That night, a precious woman was set free from the bondage that had plagued her family for generations and stepped into a dimension of God's intended freedom she had not known before.

Perhaps the most important lesson I took away from that evening was God simply asked me to listen to His voice and to obey. He clearly demonstrated He would do the rest. With merely a whisper of His word and the faith to believe, He gave me an in-depth assurance, one that has never left me to this day; every Word of God contains within it the power to bring it to pass.

Every Word of God contains within it the power to bring it to pass.

And so we come to understand, to advance the Kingdom of God and engage Christ's ministry in the spiritual realm as His responsible emissaries, we must do what He did and be sure we're saying what He said. Jesus Himself explained, *"I tell you the truth, the Son can do nothing by himself. He does only what He sees the Father doing. Whatever the Father does, the Son also does"* (John 5:19-20, *NLT*). Jesus later went on to declare, *"I don't speak on my own authority. The Father who sent me has commanded Me what to say and how to say it. And I know His commands lead to eternal life; so I say whatever the Father tells me to say"* (John 12:49-50, *NLT*).

Once again, relying on the Gospel accounts of the Lord's engagement with the darkness, we realize none of the prayers He prayed to confront the adversary were precisely alike. Jesus ongoingly sought God's wisdom and direction, waited on His timing, took authority over the enemy, and *"... cast out demons by the Spirit of God..."* (Matthew 12:28, *NKJV*). Every account offers a clear indication of the presence of the Kingdom of God. And now, the Lord invites us into His miraculous story to partner with Him in overcoming the darkness on earth, as it is in heaven.

I'm often reminded of the insightful words my pastor spoke years ago, "Delayed obedience is disobedience." The ancient languages weave the idea of obedience into the words for hearing and listening. During my seminary years, I trained and worked as an audiometrist at a local hospital and the John Tracy Clinic in Los Angeles, California. My role was to conduct hearing screenings to detect hearing loss in newborn infants and preschoolers. One of the things I came to understand in the context of my audiological education; if everything is working as God designed it, hearing is an involuntary response to sound. It is a miraculous gift of our Creator, one that we often fail to appreciate until we begin to lose it.

To listen, however, is unquestionably a very different matter. Listening is an intentional, deliberate choice that also involves our response. I believe to listen to another is a sign of respect for the one speaking and ultimately an act of submission. Most assuredly, there is no other way to experience the privilege of partnering with the action and power of God in the unseen spiritual realm and defeat the darkness except to hear, listen, and without delay, obediently follow the voice of God.

There's one more story I'd like to share with you, well, one more in this chapter anyway. I believe it's a personal experience that will provide even more clarity to the reality of our need to hear and obey God's voice in our daily, real-life engagements in spiritual warfare.

Again I had been asked to teach spiritual warfare, this time at one of our university's distance sites about six hours from my home. This particular class was presented in a modular format, providing the necessary full-quarter instruction hours in a condensed period. I taught from 8:00 a.m. until 6:00 p.m., three days in a row. The students then had the ensuing month to complete the required reading and writing assignments. An engaged group of students filled the classroom. We broke for lunch on the second day, right after I had presented my lecture on the necessity of hearing and following God's voice in spiritual warfare.

I remembered passing by a quaint little café with outdoor seating on my way from my hotel to the campus that morning. It was a lovely, sunny day, so I decided to enjoy a light lunch and some quiet time alone in their beautiful patio to reflect on the class thus far. Shortly after I was seated, I heard the piercing sound of an emergency vehicle approaching.

One of my sons-in-law is a physician and director of the emergency department and level-one trauma center in a large, metropolitan hospital. I remember he once told me he, along with all ED physicians, is more often in the position to make the most critical, quick, life and death decisions, with the least amount of patient information than anyone else in the hospital.

For years now, aware of that circumstance; whenever I hear the familiar sound of an emergency vehicle, I immediately launch into prayer. I ask God to sustain life and breath. I ask Him to give the first responders wisdom and guidance about their patients' needs and reveal their best course of action. I ask God to provide the hospital staff that would later treat the patient for His Divine insight and strategy to restore their health and wholeness. As I softly uttered the final word of my prayer, I immediately sensed God's voice. It was not an audible voice, but something I clearly and firmly perceived in my spirit saying to me, "Stop that! The prayer you just prayed is contrary to what you just rightly instructed your students never to do. You have forgotten first and foremost to inquire of Me for the way I would have you pray."

I was stunned! I thought to myself, "But God, did You hear my prayer? It's a really good prayer, don't You think?" I know—can you believe I was having this conversation with God? Again, I discerned His voice, "It's not the prayer needed right now." And so, as I had just taught my students, I inquired of the Lord, asking, "How should I pray, Father?" Again my heart sensed His whisper, "Pray the ambulance gets to the place they need to be." Without hesitation, even though I couldn't fully understand this instruction, I obediently prayed. As I pondered what had just transpired, I asked the Lord to forgive me for my arrogance and prideful assumptions that caused me to forget to apply the principle I knew so well. I finished my lunch and made my way back to class.

Driving back, I recalled the time God spoke very specifically to Phillip, saying, "*Go over and walk along beside the carriage*" (Acts 8:29, NLT). The Lord affirmed to me, "As I spoke to my people of old, I continue to speak today. Be alert and intentional to listen."

As the students gathered back together, I noticed one young man had not returned. Because of the condensed format of the class, tardiness or absences negatively impact the student's grade. Though I had never had this student in class before, it was clear from his engagement with the material that he excelled in his studies. As time went on, I grew concerned about him. Nearly an hour had passed when, with a troubled look on his face, he quietly slipped into class. So I could speak to him, I called for a break.

He assured me he was all right but was late because he had received a call from his mom as he left for lunch. With tears and a sense of urgency, she told him she had been in a car accident. Though undeniably shaken, she believed she had not sustained an injury, but it was apparent the driver of the car that struck her was not as fortunate. Someone had called 911, but the ambulance had not yet arrived, and it seemed like it was taking a very long time. While he was on the phone with her, he could hear the sound of a siren approaching. His mom quickly said, "At last, they're here! I've got to hang up." Without hesitation, he left his friends and drove to be with his mom.

After the police and ambulance had left with the injured driver, his mom explained what had transpired. The driver of the ambulance related what had happened to him had never happened to him before. Keep in mind this occurred years ago, before the accurate GPS systems we now enjoy. The ambulance was on one street by the right name, but they were supposed to be on a completely different road—bearing the same name, but Boulevard, not Street. Being from out of town, I didn't even know the name of the street my café was on. I asked my student if he was familiar with the café and was overwhelmed to discover that it was indeed on the same road the ambulance had mistakenly traveled.

I find it challenging to find the words to express how I felt at that moment. God had intentionally positioned me in that place, at that very moment, not only to pray for the emergency responders and the injured man, but to teach me once again a vital lesson. A lesson I will never forget. We simply cannot launch into prayer thinking we know what's going on. It is essential that we inquire of the Lord and heed His instruction, assured that "...*the Spirit helps us in our weakness. For we do not know what to pray for as we ought, but the Spirit himself intercedes for us...*" (Romans 8:26, *ESV*).

When class reconvened, my student and I shared the impact of the events that had transpired during our lunch break. I related the way my experience confirmed the necessity to inquire of the Holy Spirit for direction as we pray, for His will and intention to be accomplished rather than our own. Most assuredly, we simply cannot see what He sees or know what He knows. To follow God's directive is crucial in the effective engagement of spiritual warfare. He invites us to come into partnership with Him to fulfill all He desires to accomplish. An astonishing invitation and privilege, to say the least.

One last point; it's imperative that when we hear God's voice of instruction or direction, we pause to ask the question, "Lord, what do You want me to do with this revelation?" Sometimes God will give you insight that you might effectively intercede for another, like my ambulance experience. Other times, it's a revelation for you alone. Or, it may be a word that God gives you to share. If this is the case, you then need to ask, "When? Do You want me to share this now or at a later time?" As we enter into the battle in the unseen yet very real spiritual realm, there is no substitute for inquiring of the Lord and then attentively listening for His answer. Doing so is the key that enables us to align ourselves with His timing, His intention, and His purposes.

To summarize this chapter, we understand that Satan received control of the earth through deception, as man relinquished control through his disobedience. Always the case, we invariably lose something when we disobey (*see* Genesis 3).

Through disobedience, humanity will give away their freedom, health, happiness, and security. If one continues to walk in disobedience, which we know to be sin, he or she will become a slave to the enemy. We find confirmation of this reality in the question the Apostle Paul set forth in his letter to the Romans, *"Do you not know that if you present yourselves to anyone as obedient slaves, you are slaves of the one whom you obey, either of sin, which leads to death, or of obedience, which leads to righteousness?"* (Romans 6:16, *ESV*). Thankfully, this is not the end of our story.

God intends to restore humankind to the fullness of all that was in His heart and mind for us at creation. The means of our restoration came in the life, death, and resurrection of Jesus Christ. To experience the completeness of the love and freedom Jesus gave His life to provide us, we must ongoingly engage our unseen enemy. So often, it seems he opposes us at every turn. Oh, how we need to attentively listen for and follow the voice of our all-knowing God.

As we did when we began, so we conclude this chapter with the promise of Jesus, one that bears repeating; *"My sheep hear my voice, and I know them, and they follow me"* (John 10:27, *ESV*). He will speak to us, guide us, and He will, *". . .make known to me the path of life. . ."* (Psalm 16:11a, *ESV*).

Thankfully, God never asked us to engage in the ongoing battle, or life in general, for that matter, on our own. He knows our limitations and our weaknesses and has thus lovingly given us Himself in the person of His Holy Spirit. The Spirit of Truth, who will guide us, *". . .into all the truth, for He will not speak on His own authority, but whatever He hears He will speak, and He will declare to you the things that are to come"* (John 16:13, *ESV*).

God did not leave us to navigate life on our own. He lovingly gave us Himself in the person of the Holy Spirit.

Before we move on to our next chapter on authority and power, let's pause again and pray.

"Lord, give me ears to hear Your voice and a heart to obey quickly. Forgive me for the times I have failed to cease for a moment and ask for Your direction, or pridefully thought I knew best and didn't need to hear from You at all.
Let me become so familiar with Your Word that without any trace of doubt,
I will recognize its truth when You speak to my spirit.
Strengthen me to remain diligently watchful, and fill me with the confidant expectation of hearing Your voice.
Thank You, Lord, for the assurance that You are the same yesterday, today, and forever, and, as You spoke to Your people of old, You continue to speak to me today.
I love You, Lord, and am filled with gratitude as I come to understand more deeply the vastness of Your love for me and Your intention to speak to me.
Thank You for Your promise to lead me into a life of freedom

and victory over the darkness.
In turn, I ask You to empower me
to minister Your freedom
to anyone You will entrust to my care.
In the matchless name of Jesus Christ I pray, Amen."

CHAPTER SIX

THE BELIEVER'S AUTHORITY AND POWER

"And He called the twelve together and gave them power and authority over all demons and to cure diseases and He sent them out to proclaim the kingdom of God and to heal."

(Luke 9:1-2, *ESV*)

In this battle against the realms of darkness, we realize victory only as we bring the enemy to the ultimate place of true judgment: The Cross. We drive the adversary to Calvary. Herein we see the essence of prayerful spiritual warfare—to bring every issue generated by sin, self, or Satan and all his cohorts, to the place where the blood of Jesus Christ spilled, the place where the forces of darkness were, and forever will be defeated. You'll find this to be true in your personal life or as you pray for the nations of the world.

To successfully engage the battle in the spiritual realm, get the enemy on Calvary's ground. Confront him with the Cross of Christ and the blood of Jesus. "Because, where the blood was shed, that is where the power of the enemy was broken. That's where the head of the serpent was smitten (*see* Genesis 3:15)."[15] Without a doubt, Jesus' death on the cross was not a defeat. The result of Christ's victory at Calvary, "the triumph of the Crucified,"[16] was the consummate glorious triumph.

I echo my earlier statement to reinforce it; Satan cannot steal your destiny. He can only try to make you give it up. Everything God created you to be, the enemy can only attempt to deceive you into forfeiting or surrendering it. Of this you can be assured; he is relentless in that undertaking. He will never give up.

Our greatest challenge seems to be, again and again, we allow the lies from the enemy to influence our thoughts about who God is, how much He loves us and how He works in our lives. All too often, we agree with the lies he whispers about who we are as well. Thankfully, being created in the image of God, we have the unique ability to choose the thoughts we entertain. We also have the authority to stand firmly in opposition to every deception of darkness.

---

15 Jack W. Hayford, *Pursuing the Will of God* (Van Nuys: Living Way Ministries, 2002).

16 Ibid., Billheimer, 74.

Remember my discussion concerning one of the methods used to train people to recognize counterfeit money? They study authentic currency. In that same way, we want to learn the character and nature of Jesus to deepen and strengthen our foundation in His life and ministry as it relates to spiritual warfare. Let's begin by observing the way Jesus equipped His disciples for ministry: *"And He called the twelve together and gave them power and authority over all demons and to cure diseases and He sent them out to proclaim the kingdom of God and to heal"* (Luke 9:1-2, *ESV*). Jesus was very aware that as soon as His disciples began advancing the kingdom of God in preaching and healing the sick, the realms of darkness would rise in opposition.

As emissaries of The King, Jesus' disciples were charged not only to bring the message of the good news of eternity in Christ, *"to proclaim the kingdom of God,"* but *also* to change conditions on earth, *"and to heal."* In essence, Jesus gave them the mandate to bring God's Kingdom to bear on their present circumstances and on the events they would face in days ahead.

"So Jesus said to them again, 'Peace to you! As the Father has sent Me, I also send you'" (John 20:21, *NKJV*). The Lord's words can mean nothing less to us today than they meant to His disciples then. As His followers, we are His representatives, given full authority and access to His power. Why? That through our prayerful and obedient engagement in our day-to-day lives, His Divine purpose will be made manifest in every situation we face. In essence, we could also say that this is spiritual warfare defined — *"Your kingdom come, Your will be done, on earth as it is in heaven"* (Matthew 6:10, *ESV*).

To prepare His disciples for their new roles, Jesus gave them power and authority over the demonic. He sent them forth at His command and granted them the authority to act as His emissaries. To effectively do so, He equipped them with the limitless power of the Holy Spirit. Let's take a closer look at these two words: power and authority.

As used in Scripture, *authority* is the right to rule; it's positional in nature. It's a noun that carries the meaning of "leave or permission, the power or right to give orders, make decisions, and enforce obedience."[17]

Authority is the right to rule.

Dr. Neil Anderson explains it this way—Just as a policeman has the right to stop traffic at an intersection because of his position, Jesus gave His disciples the right to rule over the demonic. The One who holds all authority in heaven and on earth then granted it to His disciples (*cf.* Matthew 28:18-19).[18] Now here's one of the most critical points to remember: spiritual authority is by no means an engagement in a game of tug-of-war on a horizontal plane. It is a vertical chain of command. The Kingdom of God and the kingdom of darkness are not equal in power, might, or dominion, one being good and the other being evil, with us trapped in the middle!

When Jesus took His seat at the right hand of the Majesty in the heavens (*see* Hebrews 1:3), "He proved conclusively

---

17 *The New Oxford American Dictionary*, Oxford University Press, *s.v.* "authority," accessed March 7, 2020, https://oxfordreference.com.

18 Neil T. Anderson, *The Bondage Breaker* (Eugene: Harvest House, 1990), 59-60.

that Satan's devastation was complete, that he was utterly undone. Hell was thrown into total bankruptcy. Satan was not only stripped of his legal authority and dominion, but by an infinitely superior force he was stripped of his weapons also. But this is not all. When Jesus burst forth from that dark prison and 'ascended up on high,' all believers were raised and seated together with Him."[19] *"But God, who is rich in mercy, because of His great love with which He loved us, even when we were dead in trespasses, made us alive together with Christ ... and raised us up together, and made us sit together in the heavenly places in Christ Jesus,"* (Ephesians 2:4-6, *NKJV*).

God's Kingdom is above all of the kingdoms of this world, He has no equal rival, and He has graciously and lovingly seated us there with Him. This simple picture illustrates my point,

GOD

And those who have been made alive together with Christ (see Ephesians 2:5)

Satan and his hosts

Before we move on, there are three very significant truths we will want to remember about this vertical chain of command:

---

19 Ibid., Billheimer, 88.

1) The works of darkness cannot withstand Light;

2) The lies of darkness cannot withstand The Truth; and

3) The power of darkness cannot withstand God's power and authority and the shed blood of Jesus Christ.

It is Jesus Christ who has all authority in heaven and earth (*see* Matt. 28:18). He has entrusted and delegated His authority and power to those who serve Him, to be exercised *in His name* (*see* Luke 10:17-20).

"In His name," what does that mean? It's said so often in church, and we pray it all the time, "In the name of Jesus..." but have we ever stopped to think about what it means? Dr. Dallas Willard once explained it to me in this way: "In His name means on His behalf, under His directive, with all the power of heaven at our disposal." In this, we come to understand His name is synonymous with His mission, to seek and save the lost, to see the wounded and sick healed and the demonized delivered. "As we are one with Him in intimacy, so we become one with Him in purpose."[20]

In contrast with authority, *power* is the *ability* to rule. We recognize the word power relates to might, strength, or force. Let's consider once again the analogy of the policeman. While he has the authority to stop traffic, he really doesn't have the physical ability to do so alone. Dressed in a t-shirt and jeans, were he to merely run out onto a busy highway and stand in front of the oncoming cars, he more than likely would get run over. But if he were to come in uniform, armed, accompanied by SWAT

---

20 Francis Frangipane, *The Stronghold of God* (Lake Mary, FL: Charisma House, 1994), 69.

teams and armored vehicles, he'd now be equipped with both the authority and the power to stop nearly anything.

Power is the ability to rule.

Similarly, we recognize it's Christ's power that goes before us and with us, not our own. He doesn't send us into battle empty-handed either; instead, He has given us His armor and His weapons to equip and protect us so that we may effectively engage in the unseen war. That while we are human, God assures us, "...*we don't wage war as humans do. We use God's mighty weapons, not worldly weapons, to knock down the strongholds of human reasoning and to destroy false arguments*" (2 Corinthians 10:4-5, *NLT*).

In a military parade, weapons lend impressiveness. However, we have to acknowledge that as the warrior faces a relentless enemy, one who refuses appeasement, the soldier who fights wins, and fighting involves using a weapon. "Unused weapons do not inflict casualties on the enemy nor win wars. Therefore the ability and the will to use weapons is what warfare is all about. It is not enough to give mental assent to the fact spiritual warfare is going on. Passivity toward our enemy is what the devil wants from us and is his trick to cool the ardor of God's men of war."[21]

God is calling us to rise with a warrior-heart pounding within us, willing to dress in the entirety of His armor (*see* Ephesians 6:11-19) and implement His spiritual weapons, that victory may become a reality. "Jesus puts the initiative

---

21 R. Arthur Mathews, *Born For Battle: 31 Studies on Spiritual Warfare* (Singapore: Overseas Missionary Fellowship, 1978), 54.

for action into the hands of His people and promises that when they act, Heaven will endorse."[22]

We learn from Christ's encounter with the enemy in the wilderness (*see* Luke 4:1-13) that one of our most effective spiritual weapons is the Word of Truth given to us in Scripture. The Blood of Jesus and the word of our testimony (*see* Revelation 12:11) will overcome the darkness, as will the Sword of His Spirit (*see* Luke 4:1-13 and Ephesians 6:13-18). Worship and praise are astonishingly mighty weapons of warfare (*see* Joshua 6), for Jesus inhabits the praises of His people (*see* Psalm 22:3). And one of the most powerful weapons of all is the love of God. His love poured through us to one another, for it is God's *"perfect love [that] casts out. . ."* (1 John 4:18a, *ESV*).

The effective utilization of God's spiritual weapons is most assuredly dependent upon our understanding that our paramount responsibility is to prayerfully inquire of the Holy Spirit for the revelation of His strategy and timing related to their use. The Holy Spirit will faithfully distribute His gifts of faith, wisdom, knowledge, discerning of spirits, and the working of miracles as He directs us in the robust implementation of His weapons (*see* 1 Corinthians 10:7-11). For a vast number of reasons, the heat of battle is not the time for us to guess or rely on our own understanding; we need the Lord's perspective (*see* Proverbs 3:5-6 *and* Colossians 1:9).

By faith, God transforms our weaknesses into strength, that we will become strong in battle and conquer the influence of the kingdom of darkness in our lives (*see* Hebrews 11:33-

---

22 Ibid., Mathews, 57.

34). As we seek and obey God's instructions, He commands us today just as He commanded Joshua, *"Be strong and courageous! Do not be afraid or discouraged. For the Lord your God is with you wherever you go"* (Joshua 1:9b, *NLT*).

Christ delegated responsibility in giving His disciples authority. He also equipped them with the fullness of His power to effectively accomplish the task of imposing His victory at Calvary onto the state of affairs in the world in which they lived. He does the same for us now. Jesus Christ is the fountainhead of both power and authority, and He has determined His Church shall be the agent to enforce His will. Once again, declaring on earth as it is in heaven, *"so that through the church the manifold wisdom of God might now be made known to the rulers and authorities in the heavenly places"* (Ephesians 3:10, *ESV*).

May we never underestimate the absolute importance of the Church in God's design. While God needs nothing, His Word informs us that "He has chosen voluntarily to limit himself in order that the Church shares in His reign. It is true that the Body cannot function without the Head. It is just as true that the Head, by His own choice, will not function without the Body. Both are important to the accomplishment of His plan."[23] (*see* Ephesians 1:22-23).

"Without knowing who you are in Christ and understanding your God-given authority in Him, you have no authority. And you certainly have no fight."[24] Consider with me the

---

23 Ibid., Billheimer, 89.

24 John Ramirez, *Armed and Dangerous: The Ultimate Battle Plan for Targeting and Defeating the Enemy.* (Minneapolis: Chosen, a division of Baker Publishing Group, 2017),120.

account we read of in the Book of Acts, one that tells us what happened when several men attempted to fight the forces of evil without legitimate God-given authority. *"They tried to use the name of the Lord Jesus in their incantation, saying, 'I command you in the name of Jesus, whom Paul preaches, to come out! ... The evil spirit replied, 'I know Jesus, and I know Paul, but who are you?' Then the man with the evil spirit leaped on them, overpowered them, and attacked them with such violence that they fled from the house, naked and battered"* (Acts 19:13-16, *NLT*).

Let us not be confused. On our own, we don't have the authority or power to confront the demonic realm. It doesn't come based on our education, calling, or experience—it attends our personal relationship with Christ. Paul's admonition to the church in Philippi still stands to admonish us today, *"We rely on what Christ Jesus has done for us. We put no confidence in human effort"* (Philippians 3:3b, *NLT*). Our authority is given to us by Christ, and the power is His and His alone.

In moving out in God's authority and power, perhaps the most important thing I will share with you is this—it's critical to remember the human vulnerability to pride, which comes with the sense of dominion over the powers of darkness. We would be wise to heed the warning of Dr. C. Peter Wagner, that "If we go into spiritual warfare and expect to have God's power without humility on our part, we are in trouble. ... Effective spiritual warfare requires a delicate balance of weakness and power. The minute we begin to think we are doing it ourselves, we become vulnerable to the enemy's attack."[25]

25 C. Peter Wagner, *Warfare Prayer: How to Seek God's Power and Protection in the Battle to Build His Kingdom* (Ventura, CA: Regal Books, 1992), 188.

You may recall the Gospel account of the time the Lord appointed seventy-two to go before Him as His ambassadors. Not sent to sow seed, but to bring in the harvest (*see* Luke 10:2). They came back filled with excitement, declaring, *"Even the demons are subject to us in Your name"* (Luke 10:17b, *NKJV*). Jesus instructed that the valid point of ministry is to rejoice that your name is written in heaven. He wasn't saying, "Just be glad you're saved and not that the demons are subject to you." Jesus declared it is the inscription of your name in heaven that gives you the credentials to move in the authority you do.

"Ours is the privilege ~ His is the power." Dr. Jack W. Hayford

It is imperative to recognize in every battle, we draw our authority from the fact we are the Kingdom of Heaven's representatives. We are to be ever on guard against pride. Know this, dear reader, if we think for a moment that the enemy flees because of us, as C. S. Lewis once concluded, we may as well be prideful about the color of our eyes. When you see the demons yield, be very clear it is the result of being locked into the power of Almighty God. Jesus Himself reminds us to rejoice in the reality that our names are written in heaven—and that's why the demons are subject to our prayers—the only reason (*see* Luke 10:17-20).

I was recently forewarned of this truth by Max Lucado.

> *Do you see a person wise in their own eyes? There is more hope for a fool than for them* (Proverbs 26:12). God hates pride. How do we explain God's abhorrence of the haughty heart? Simple. God resists the proud because

the proud resist God. Arrogance stiffens the knee so it will not kneel, hardens the heart so it will not admit to sin. The heart of pride never confesses, never repents, never asks for forgiveness. Indeed, the arrogant never feel the need for forgiveness. Pride is the hidden reef that shipwrecks the soul.

Pride comes at a high price. Don't pay it. Choose instead to stand on the offer of grace. *God resists the proud, but gives grace to the humble* (1 Peter 5:5). Isn't it easy to see why? Humility is happy to do what pride will not. The humble heart is quick to acknowledge the need for God, eager to confess sin, willing to kneel before heaven's mighty hand.[26]

Glenn Burris, past President of The Foursquare Church, observed in conversation, "Pride is the carbon monoxide of sin. It silently and slowly kills you without you even knowing." May we be reminded even Jesus learned obedience in humble submission to God (*See* Philippians 2:8). We find our strength in battle in our submission to the Lord. In humility, Christ clarified His submission with these words, *"I don't speak on My own authority. The Father who sent Me has commanded Me what to say and how to say it"* (John 12:49, NLT). We observe throughout the Gospels, Jesus didn't speak until He heard the Father's voice. Only then did He confidently move in humble obedience and authoritative power.

Beloved, Jesus has entrusted us with His authority and His power. Once again, we must decide whether or not we are going to live it out. I realize there are times, even

---

26 Max Lucado, "Why God Hates Pride," Daily Devotionals, February 27, 2020, https://maxlucado.com/listen/why-god-hates-pride/

after we come to know who we are in Christ and face the adversary's pressures, we can forget our position. This is why we need to remain ever alert to God's voice and the leading of the Holy Spirit.

We earlier discovered the keys of God's Kingdom give us access and right of entry, yet are of no value unless we pick them up and use them. In the same way, merely knowing about the authority God gives, coupled with the awesome power He makes available, is of little benefit unless we choose to engage both. We can either lower the standard of Scripture to align with our life's experience thus far, or we can decide today to raise the standard of our life to align with God's Word. If we choose to move out with confident expectation, we will experience His glory, His life, His freedom, and the victory of His Kingdom rule in our life's journey here on earth.

We can either lower the standard of Scripture to align with our life's experience thus far, or we can decide today to raise the standard of our life to align with God's Word.

Living in God's authority and power refers to the truth of God's Word and the truth about our everyday lives. There is a need for our uncompromised integrity. It doesn't mean we will never fail, but when we do, we heed His gentle correction, learn from our experience, and respond quickly and appropriately. It's a matter of being forthright and honest with our heavenly Father, to come before Him and receive His forgiveness and cleansing and let our failures become that which strengthen us (*see* 1 John 1:8-9). Once again, the choice is ours.

From here, we're going to move into the practical application of the pursuit of our freedom; but before we do, will you again partner with me in prayer?

"Father, thank You once again for the precious gift of
Your Son, Jesus Christ.
As Your follower, I thank You, Lord, for the authority
You have given me and the assurance that the infinite
power of the Holy Spirit will accompany me as I live
to be Your emissary on Earth. I humbly surrender to
Your leading and promise to obey Your directives. With
a new, more in-depth understanding of my position in
You, strengthen me to never again turn from the enemy
in fear as he seeks to assault me
and shift my focus away from You.
I humbly ask You to empower me to run to my
adversary, not away from him.
In Your Name may I prayerfully destroy the devices he
employs against me, my family, my home, my finances,
my health, my ministry, my country, and everything
else You have entrusted to my care.
Forgive me, Lord, for any place I have given
to pride in my life, thus failing to walk
in humble submission to You.
I renounce any opportunity I have given to the darkness
in my sin, and refuse further association
with pride and self-will.
Strengthen me, first in character and faith, then in
privilege and power, that I may effectively enforce Your
glorious victory at Calvary,
partnering with You to destroy the works of the devil.

Lead me by Your Holy Spirit, that I may in true humility serve Your intention and fulfill Your purposes all the days of my life.
In the name of my Lord and Savior, Jesus Christ, Amen."

CHAPTER SEVEN

THE PURSUIT
OF FREEDOM

---

*"The reason the Son of God appeared
was to destroy the works of the devil."*

(1 John 3:8, *ESV*)

Over the years, I'm often asked, "Can a Christian have
a demon?" And if so, "How can the follower of Christ be
set free?" These questions, and the related uncertainties,
have caused division in the Church down through the
centuries. While skepticism remains within the Church
today, an observable rise in occult and New Age practices
makes it increasingly difficult for the Church to ignore
the subjects of demonic influence and deliverance. People
crying out for the freedom only Jesus Christ can give
surround us everywhere we go. In this chapter, we'll look
to the Scripture to discover the answers.

There is a need for balance and wisdom. "Thoughtful Christians realize they need to exercise discernment between psychological problems—for which the patient needs counseling, emotional healing, psychiatric help or medication—and the presence of a real demonic entity in the person, in which case deliverance is called for."[27] It is a call to an element of ministry that Jesus Himself engaged, one for which there is no substitute. Further, if we believe that Jesus' commission to His disciples was to *"Heal the sick, raise the dead, cleanse the lepers, cast out demons"* (Matthew 10:8a, *NASB*), then we must also believe this remains His commission to His followers today.

In the pages ahead, we'll investigate what God said through the Apostle Paul on this matter, beginning with his question to the church in Rome, *"Do you not know that if you present yourselves to anyone as obedient slaves, you are slaves of the one whom you obey, either of sin, which leads to death, or of obedience, which leads to righteousness?"* (Romans 6:16, *ESV*). Though I wish it were true, it's been my experience, and perhaps yours as well, old habits don't just fall away once a person enters into a personal relationship with Jesus Christ.

There are also situations when followers of Christ unwittingly allow themselves to drift into sinful behaviors, thinking, "Well, just this once, it's really not that bad, and I can stop anytime." In the words of Pastor Jack Hayford, "Submission to sin is not necessarily an action where a person bows the knee and says, 'I will.' It's where a person comes to a place where he allows himself to be

---

27 Francis MacNutt, *Deliverance from Evil Spirits: A Practical Manual* (Grand Rapids: Chosen, A division of Baker Publishing Group, 2009), 18.

exposed to it."[28] You wouldn't expect to spend hours in the bright, hot sunshine, unprotected by a hat or sunscreen, and return without a sunburn. In that same way, you can't expect to go out into our current fallen world, unprotected by the resources God makes available to us, and return without what could be described as a "hell burn." Because we live in the unseen yet very real, spiritual realm, we can be sure that we will be exposed to demonic activity in our daily lives, and it will affect us.

Deliverance is a call to Jesus, who is The Deliverer. "A major reason Jesus took on human flesh was to free us from demonic influence. For Him it was no side issue, no minor ministry. His title is Savior because He came to free us from evil."[29] As I've earlier noted, Jesus came to "...*destroy the works of the devil*" (1 John 3:8, *ESV*). "Any place that hell makes inroads—in our lives, our homes, our thoughts, our habits—Jesus comes to break that power and to set us free. By His cross and His resurrection, He distinguishes Himself as Lord above all."[30]

2 Corinthians 1:10 reveals Jesus *"delivered us from such a deadly peril, and He will deliver us. On Him we have set our hope that He will deliver us again."* The follower of Christ comes to understand that salvation is an instant, miraculous gift of God's love and grace—we become a new creation (*see* 1 Corinthians 5:17). The restoration of our soul, however, is a process. God welcomes us into a new realm, that of His Kingdom, setting us on a path of

---

28 Jack W. Hayford, *The Way Demon Angels Trick, Trap, and Trample* (Van Nuys: Living Way Ministries, 1995), 41.

29 Ibid., MacNutt, 19.

30 Ibid., Hayford, 49.

renewal, healing, and deliverance from the residue of our old life and the effects of the sinful world.

Christ brings us *"...out of darkness into His marvelous light"* (1 Peter 2:9b, *ESV*). Beloved, that's the most significant change of address you will ever make!! It's a move that creates and opens a new world of possibilities and opportunities to all who believe and receive Jesus Christ as their Lord and Savior. It will be an ongoing process of experiencing the love of God, filling us with His life, healing, and the freedom to step into all He intends for us going forward.

Please pause with me for a moment. I never want to deal with the demonic without addressing the security of the believer's life in Jesus. *"He who is in you is greater than he who is in the world"* (1 John 4:4, *ESV*). Oh, how I praise God for this reality! The moment we chose to engage life as a follower of Christ, the greater One, preeminent over anything we might encounter on earth, came to live in you and me, and He lovingly offers the fullness of His life and liberty to each of us. Thank you, Lord! In light of this truth, we are further assured, "There is nothing that Jesus used to defeat Satan that is not available to us. Therefore, victory is as attainable for us as it was for Him."[31]

Now, have a look with me at 2 Timothy 2:17-21 (*ESV*). There's little doubt Paul wrote this letter during his second Roman imprisonment, shortly before his imminent execution. While he wrote to encourage and admonish his young co-worker, his main concern was for the Church's welfare. The apostle urges his fellow believers to safeguard the Gospel as a sacred deposit committed to them.

---

31 Ibid., Mathews, 21.

During this season, there were two men, Hymenaeus and Philetus, whose teachings had drifted from the truth, and it was spreading like cancer through the Church. The Word goes on to explain, *"Nevertheless, the solid foundation of God stands, having this seal: 'The Lord knows those who are His'"* (v. 19). These men were followers of Christ, having God's seal on their lives. As Paul continues, he instructs them and all believers, clearly stating, *"Let everyone who names the name of the Lord depart from iniquity"* (v. 19b).

Iniquity is a strong word meaning lawlessness, wickedness, and violating the law of God. It's about disorder apart from God's order. When we disobey God's laws, it's imperative to understand there will always be consequences that bring death. We often think only in terms of physical death, but what about death to hopes and dreams, or an emotional or spiritual death? This is not merely a call to obedience beloved, but a call to God's love and liberty. Let's keep moving ahead.

2 Timothy 2:20 continues, *"Now in a great house there are not only vessels of gold and silver but also of wood and clay, some for honorable use, some for dishonorable."* Thankfully, this is not a predestined supposition. God predetermines no one for dishonor or to be degraded from fulfilling His purposes in and through their life.

Stay with me; it gets good here! Verse 21 offers the solution, *"If you keep yourself pure, you will be a special utensil for honorable use. Your life will be clean, and you will be ready for the Master to use you for every good work"* (2 Timothy 2:21, NLT). This verse provides proof we are dealing with something other than salvation, for we realize we cannot, in our own strength, cleanse ourselves from our sin. Nothing but the blood of Jesus accomplished the forgiveness of sin, once and for all. Amen and amen! However, it is up to us to take personal responsibility to engage the process Christ offers to restore our souls.

How do we do that? God clearly instructs us through Paul's earlier letter to the Ephesian church, "...*You must no longer walk as the Gentiles do, in the futility of their minds*" (Ephesians 4:17b, *ESV*), "*and give no opportunity to the devil*" (Ephesians 4:27). These two Scriptures would be meaningless exhortations if it were not possible for the believer to give the devil an opportunity. And how do we provide him with opportunity? We sin. These passages teach us that sin, when yielded to, will open the door that welcomes the enemy in upon us. Simply yet profoundly stated, we must refuse to walk in the futile ways of unbelievers.

The Greek word for "opportunity" here, or as it reads in some translations, "place" is "*topos.*" It's the root of our English word "topographic," which describes detailed geographic mapping. It "emphasizes that believers can actually give ground in their lives to satanic control. This is a warning against theologized suppositions that argue against the possibility that demonic vexing or oppression may succeed with Christians. But the surrounding commands balance the issue (Ephesians 4:17–5:14), making clear that responsible believers cannot glibly blame the devil for the sin they yield to in carnal disobedience."[32]

---

32 Jack W. Hayford, Ephesians, Notes 4:27, *Spirit Filled Life Bible*, General Ed, Jack W. Hayford (Nashville: Thomas Nelson, 2002),1652.

To ensure we're on the same page, let's take a quick look at what sin is. I believe we're on solid ground when we align ourselves with Jesus' definition of sin. He said, "*A nobleman was called away to a distant empire to be crowned king and then return. Before he left, he called together ten of his servants and divided among them ten pounds of silver, saying, 'Invest this for me while I am gone.' But his people hated him and sent a delegation after him to say, 'We do not want him to be our king.'*" (Luke 19:12-14, *NLT*).

The insightful words of Max Lucado shed more light on Jesus' parable, "To sin is to state, 'God, I do not want you to be my king.' Sin shouts, 'I want to run my own life, thank you very much!' Sin is insurrection of the highest order, and you are an insurrectionist. So am I. 'But,' oh that wonderful word but, 'God demonstrates His own love toward us, in that while we were sinners, Christ died for us' (Romans 5:8). Christ died to set the insurrectionist free—you and me—free."[33]

Getting back to the battle, the Greek word for demon activity in our lives is "*daimonizomai*," which means "to be vexed with a demon." But when this Greek word is translated as "possessed," we somehow get the idea that the person involved *belongs* to a demon or demons. This interpretation simply is not the case in the life of a follower of Christ.

Within our current culture, the word "*daimonizomai*" would carry a much clearer meaning if we would translate it as "an overwhelming demonic influence" rather than "demon

---

33 Max Lucado, *God is With You Every Day* (Nashville: Thomas Nelson, 2015), May 24.

possession." I once heard it said this way; demons do not possess or own a follower of Christ. God owns them. They are His creatures, and He is their judge. If they inhabit His people, they have only squatters' rights. Though simply stated, it communicates an absolute, unqualified truth.

That being said, the reality that demon spirits can affect us is evident in Scripture (looking at the Gospel of Matthew alone, *cf.* Matthew 4:24; 8:16,28-34; 9:32-34; 10:1,8; 12:22,43-45; 15:22-28; 17:14-21). When a demon enters a person, it can influence the person's thoughts and behaviors. If Christ lives there, literal demon possession is not possible, but unfortunately, demonic influence is. Demons work against a Christian through the soul (one's mind, will, and emotions). They can do so even if the person has a relationship with Jesus Christ, which is why we must constantly resist the enemy.

Returning to 2 Timothy, Paul instructs us, *"...flee youthful passions (lusts) and pursue righteousness, faith, love, and peace, along with those who call on the Lord from a pure heart. Have nothing to do with foolish, ignorant controversies; you know that they breed quarrels. And the Lord's servant must not be quarrelsome, but kind to everyone..."* (2 Timothy 2:22-24a, *ESV*).

He's talking to people "in the great house," the believer! These are God's children, living in the glory and certainty of His love, but a people in need of cleansing nonetheless. His family, *"...patiently enduring evil, correcting his opponents with gentleness. [That] God may perhaps grant them repentance leading to a knowledge of the truth, and they may escape from the snare of the devil, after being captured by him to do his will"* (2 Timothy 2:24b-26, *ESV*).

Christ will not coerce us by force. We are each responsible for what takes place in our hearts and thoughts, knowing that our thoughts lead to our actions. To combat the enemy's work against our souls, we must choose to submit to the Lordship of Jesus Christ by denying sin and obeying God's Word. When believers give place to the darkness, it creates the inability to move in freedom. We then find ourselves reacting rather than responding to the circumstances of our lives. Thankfully, the Lord loves us too much to leave us that way. God deals respectfully and gently with us as He calls us to repentance and extends His offer of freedom, a freedom that brings us back to a place of choice.

Thinking about ministry to one another, we need to remember we serve everyone with the same love, gentleness, and respect that Christ extends to us. It's vital to maintain the ministry perspective that understands we are not the deliverer; we minister God's deliverance. You and I don't heal anyone; we minister God's healing. Try as we might, we can't save anyone; we express the salvation Gospel of Jesus Christ. The Word of God is alive, and its power brings light to the darkness. (*see* Hebrews 4:11-14; 1 Thessalonians 5:23).

As we continue our discussion concerning repentance from 2 Timothy, we understand repentance is more than simply regret; it's turning away from sin. It involves changing one's thinking, that they may know the truth, the Truth that will set them free (*cf.* John 8:32). Repentance in Greek is the word "*metanoia*," which carries the meaning of a person making a U-turn, a complete reversal in opinion or actions, and heading back to God. [34] It's much like the Hebrew word *"teshuvah,"* which describes repentance's personal and emotional process. In essence, it is to return to the Lord.[35] Most often, I've experienced the turn to be the most challenging part, but God lovingly extends His grace for the process.

Repentance is more than simply regret; it's turning away from sin.

The enemy can also get a foothold in a believer's life (or non-believer for that matter) through life circumstances, and more significantly, our responses to them. Common entry points include youthful lusts, heartbreak, abandonment, disappointment, dominating fear, rejection, parental neglect, poverty, immorality, and generational curses, to name a few. At these times, the enemy intrudes where there has perhaps been no intentional sin on our part. Traumatic events such as abuse (physical, emotional, or sexual), a car accident, a parental breakup, or seasons of life such as menopause (men and women), puberty, and pregnancy are particularly vulnerable times in life when our adversary will seize every opportunity to trap us.

Word curses, especially those spoken over us by authority figures, such as "You're so stupid" or "You never do anything right," or even curses we have spoken against ourselves, will give an opportunity to the devil.

---

34 *THAYER'S GREEK LEXICON,* Electronic Database. Copyright © 2002, 2003, 2006, 2011 by Biblesoft, Inc. All rights reserved. Used by permission. BibleSoft.com

35 Rabbi David Fohrman, https://www.alephbeta.org/ © 2019 Aleph Beta, Hoffberger Institute for Text Study, Inc.

In Proverbs 6:2, we read, *"You are snared by the words of your mouth; You are taken by the words of your mouth."* Graciously, God faithfully offers His solution in Proverbs 12:6b, *"But the mouth of the upright will deliver them"* (Proverbs 12:6b, *NKJV*). Here we are again; the choice is ours.

I don't know about you, but I am often my own worst enemy! Before we speak degrading or disparaging words about ourselves or others, we simply must begin to give careful consideration to their impact, for the devil is no respecter of persons. He has absolutely no compassion related to who he will take advantage of or when he will do it. There is no doubt our adversary can and will relentlessly seize every opportunity to entrap humanity.

At this point, I'd like to take us back to the question we began this chapter with, "Can a Christian have a demon?" The truths we've just investigated expose the fact the answer is "Yes," yet perhaps this isn't the question that matters most after all. The more pressing question remaining before us is, "How can we personally experience the freedom Christ gave His life to give us?"

The beginning point is a personal relationship with Jesus Christ. Responding to Thomas's question, *"'...how can we know the way?' Jesus said to him, 'I Am the way, the truth, and the life. No one comes to the Father except through Me'"* (John 14:5-6, *NKJV*).

"He who loves Me will be loved by My Father, and I will love him and manifest Myself to him" (John 14:21b, *NKJV*).

The authority of the name of the Lord Jesus has been granted only to those who have a personal relationship with Him (*see* Mark 16:17 and Luke 10:17-20). It is only "in Christ" we have His authority and access to the power of the Holy Spirit to achieve victory over the darkness.

Be warned, dear reader, any attempt to engage the demonic realm in your own strength will most assuredly result in you becoming a casualty of war, just as were the itinerant exorcists, I earlier referenced, and we read about in Acts 19:13-17.

> *"Then some of the itinerant Jewish exorcists took it upon themselves to call the name of the Lord Jesus over those who had evil spirits, saying, 'We exorcise you by the Jesus whom Paul preaches.' ... And the evil spirit answered and said, 'Jesus I know, and Paul I know; but who are you?' Then the man in whom the evil spirit was leaped on them, overpowered them, and prevailed against them, so that they fled out of that house naked and wounded. This became known both to all Jews and Greeks dwelling in Ephesus; and fear fell on them all, and the name of the Lord Jesus was magnified."*

Prayers offered and ministry attempted by faith and in the name of Jesus must be in accord with His nature and His purpose (*see* John 14:13) for, "To know the ways of God is to become knowledgeable of the motives of His heart and intimate with the secrets of His passions."[36]

Think back with me to Chapter Two and the tuna salad story I told, revealing our real dilemma and how often we can misdiagnose it. My friend, if you have not yet come to

---

36 Ibid., Frangipane, 10.

the place in your spiritual journey when you acknowledge you're no different than anyone else in life—a sinner in need of a Savior—you currently stand in life's most significant dilemma. All of us have disobeyed God; it's not a new problem! It's a dilemma stretching back to Adam and Eve. It's disobedience, plain and simple, which the Word of God calls sin. In Paul's letter to the Romans, he describes sin's consequence, *"The wages of sin is death"* (Romans 6:23a, *ESV*). The only possible response consistent with God's righteous and just character is a penalty; one, if left unaddressed, you will carry with you into eternity.

Graciously, concurrent with God's holiness and justice, He is lovingly compassionate. God never intended, nor wanted, His creation to live apart from Him or meet our deserved fate. He alone offers the only remedy. I stand in awe of the reality that He is a reach-down, step into our world God of rescue. And what is His remedy to our dilemma? It is nothing less than His passionate, pursuing, unfailing, and unconditional love for each one of us. Scripture reveals that *"God so loved the world that He gave His one and only Son, [Jesus Christ], that whoever believes in Him shall not perish, but have eternal life"* (John 3:16, *NLT*). Jesus affirmed God's plan by assuring us, *"I came that they may have life and have it abundantly"* —a complete life, full of purpose (John 10:10b, *ESV*).

Then, as I've just mentioned, God asks us to honestly acknowledge our dilemma with the understanding that the result of sin is death and spiritual separation from God (*see* Romans 6:23). He asks us to humbly confess we have sinned and are thus living separated from God.

Now for the good news! Jesus died in our place; He paid the penalty in full, so we could enjoy a relationship with God and be with Him forever. *"God demonstrates His own love toward us, in that while we were yet sinners, Christ died for us"* (Romans 5:8, *NKJV*). But it didn't end with His substitutionary death on the cross. Christ's body laid in a tomb, and according to Scripture, on the third day, He rose to life again (*see* 1 Corinthians 15:3-4). Jesus still lives today and is the fulfillment of God's perfect plan to restore relationship with humanity. He is the only way to enter into a personal relationship with God.

There's nothing we can do to earn salvation; we are saved by God's grace when we, in faith, believe in His Son, Jesus Christ. The Father knows you and deeply loves you. He longs for you to experience the transformation from a life-and-death story into a role in His grand story—one of life death and life again!

While salvation cannot be earned, it can be rejected. Rejection is a remedy of one's own choosing, one that will lead to a much deeper dilemma. If you would like to receive God's forgiveness and enter into a personal relationship with Him right now, or maybe you've walked away from God, and you'd like to return to an intimate relationship with Him, I ask you to pray the following prayer with me. There's no better time than the present.

"Dear Lord Jesus, I believe in Your love for me. I thank You, Lord, for the gift of forgiveness of sin You offer me now. I know I have sinned against You, and I am sorry.

*I ask for Your forgiveness. I believe You shed Your blood
on the cross to pay the penalty for my sins and that
You rose from the dead.
Jesus, because You are alive forever, I ask You to come
into my heart and live with me. I choose today to trust
and follow You as my Lord and my Savior. Guide my
life and empower me to do Your will.
In Your matchless name I pray, Amen."*

If you have prayed this for the first time or prayed it as
a point of rededication, you now walk the path of life
accompanied by the Lord God Himself who promises,
"I am with you always, even to the end of the age" (Matthew
28:20b, *NKJV*). He has called you to go into all the world
to share the Gospel and to make disciples. At His direction
and in faith believing, His commission includes the
privileged invitation to partner with Him to heal the sick,
raise the dead, cleanse the lepers, and cast out demons
(*see* Matthew 10:7-8; 28:19-20; Mark 16:15-18). You are His
hands extended to a world in desperate need, and oh, what
an astonishing adventure I know you will discover it to be.

CHAPTER EIGHT

MULTIPLE STREAMS OF DELIVERANCE

*"And you shall know the truth,
and the truth shall make you free."*

(John 8:32, *NKJV*)

As you continue to navigate this book, may I encourage you not merely to read; but instead consider the possibility of learning and teaching? God doesn't set us free merely for freedom's sake; He calls us to equip ourselves to minister His life, truth, and freedom to all those He will bring into our lives (*see* Matthew 28:19-20; Acts 1:8). Freedom does begin with you though, so let's continue by investigating some of the varied ways God leads us into a life walked out in the full release of His glory and power.

When I first learned about the ministry of "deliverance,"
I assumed it meant freedom from the powers of darkness.
And it does. Yet as the years have gone by, I have come
to understand that truthfully everything God does is
deliverance! Salvation is deliverance from the penalty of
our sin. Healing is deliverance from the consequence of
sickness and disease, whether it is physical, emotional, or
spiritual. And the casting out of darkness is deliverance
from the heinous grip of our adversary, the devil.

Every element of deliverance Jesus offers us is a stepping
"out of" all that has kept us from stepping *"into"* an eternal
relationship with Him, an astonishing relationship wherein
we will discover and enjoy the fullness of His intended
dominion and destiny for our lives. The Apostle Peter
affirms this truth in his First Epistle wherein he conveys
to us, *"But you are a chosen generation, a royal priesthood,
a holy nation, His own special people, that you may proclaim
the praises of Him who called you out of darkness into His
marvelous light;"* (1 Peter 2:9, *NKJV*).

Throughout over forty years of involvement in deliverance
ministries, I have met people worldwide who believed
the only way to experience freedom from the realm of
darkness is to battle the demonic in confrontational prayer.
In light of God's Word, that simply does not hold true. I've
learned and experienced there are multiple ways the Lord
delivers us.

First, the delivering stream of growth in Truth, the Word of God

There is unprecedented power inherent in the Word of
God. We mature in our relationship with the Lord as we

hear, read, teach, and memorize Scripture. Listen to Jesus as He spoke to His followers, *"If you abide in My word, you are My disciples indeed. And you shall know the truth, and the truth shall make you free"* (John 8:31b-32, *NKJV*). As I've previously maintained, every word of God contains within it the power to bring it to pass. Authentically engaging the truth of God's Word will bring freedom to your life.

The word "disciple" carries within its meaning "a disciplined one," also to be "a follower." This passage of Scripture compels us to seek the answer to the question, "Who are Jesus' disciples, His disciplined ones, to whom He makes this promise of freedom?" Pastor Jon Courson describes them this way, "Those who continue in, take heed to, and make a high priority of His Word. And it is as they comprehend the truth of the Word that they are free— freely, truly free."[37] Jesus' prayer to The Father for His disciples still reaches to those of us who are His disciples today, *"Make them holy by your truth; teach them your word, which is truth"* (John 17:17, *NLT*). As we learn and walk in the truth of God's Word, our lives will be transformed, and chains of bondage will be broken.

As we learn and walk in the truth of God's Word our lives will be transformed, and chains of bondage will be broken.

While on the journey through the pages of this book with me, it's my hope you've come to understand the reality that when we sin, we give the enemy a foothold in our lives. Conversely, when we embrace the truths of God's

---

37 Jon Courson, *John Courson's Application Commentary: The New Testament* (Nashville: Thomas Nelson, Inc., 2003), 508.

Word, not only will we experience victory over the lies of darkness, we will also discover that we've been equipped and empowered to refuse sin in our lives and walk in freedom in the future. Listen to the Divine admonition of David, *"How can a young man cleanse his way? By taking heed according to Your word. With my whole heart I have sought You; Oh, let me not wander from Your commandments! Your word I have hidden in my heart, that I might not sin against You"* (Psalm 119:9-11, *NKJV*).

Over the years, I have sought to find God in Scripture. Only quite recently, it dawned on me that the Bible is more truly a history of the many ways God finds me. The search has been His rather than my own, or mine only because it first was His. As the author of the Book of Hebrews reminds us, *"The word of God is living and powerful..."* (Hebrews 4:12a, *NKJV*). The Scripture is the self-revelation of God Himself, by the power of the Holy Spirit, each word breathed from His heart and mind to the pens of men of His choosing. Every time we prayerfully open our Bibles, humbly seeking to know God more deeply, or when we sit under trustworthy teaching of His Word, God's life-giving, transformational power becomes available to us. All that He promises within the pages of Scripture will become personal to us.

God Himself makes this truth clear to us as He spoke through the prophet Isaiah, *"The rain and snow come down from the heavens and stay on the ground to water the earth. They cause the grain to grow, producing seed for the farmer and bread for the hungry. It is the same with my word. I send it out, and it always produces fruit. It will accomplish all I want it to, and it will prosper everywhere I send it"* (Isaiah 55:10-11, *NLT*). Not "maybe," not "it might now and then;" but it will accomplish all that God Himself intends for it to, making His word the most compelling force in all of creation.

"'Is not My word like a fire?' says the Lord, 'And like a hammer that breaks the rock in pieces?'" (Jeremiah 23:29, NKJV)

Over and over again, the life and ministry of Jesus demonstrated the power in His Word, power backed by Divine displays for all to witness. Luke records such a moment, *"Then they were all amazed and spoke among themselves, saying, 'What a word this is! For with authority and power He commands the unclean spirits, and they come out'"* (Luke 4:36, *NKJV, see also Luke 4:32*).

The stream of God's love

Another way I've experienced God's delivering power is through what I would call the ministry of love. The word "ministry" refers to helping or serving one another. Often, our greatest act of service is to genuinely and unconditionally love another person. Indeed the quintessential description of God's nature is love, and to love as He loves is to offer the assistance, care, and concern that will restore a person to wholeness. Scripture informs us that *"Perfect love casts out..."* (1 John 4:18, *NKJV*), and it's not just fear that gets swept away, for this complete expression of God's love opposes and casts out every work of our adversary.

Never minimize the power of community. When we gather in the presence of the love of God, where His truth is being spoken and taught, people will be set free. In addition to sanctification, points of bondage in one's life residual to their past will be overthrown and melted away.

Sadly, the understanding of love has become vastly diminished in our current culture. To express the love of God means to act for one's good, the good of another, at times over and above our own desires. We live out our love for God by our love for people. Jesus said we would be known as His disciples "...*if you have love for one another*" (John 13:35, *NKJV*).

The worst thing love can be thought to mean is, "If you love me, you'll do what I want." Most assuredly, this kind of selfish, self-centered thinking will only bring disaster to a relationship. In glorious contrast, when the unconditional, selfless, self-giving love of God is freely poured forth (*see* "*agape*" as in Romans 5:5), it always seeks the good of the other person, without asking for anything in return. This unconquerable love contains within it God's power to cleanse, deliver and set the captive free.

The stream of a Spirit-filled walk in worship

Yet another pathway to freedom is to walk and worship in the Spirit of God. The entire chapter of Romans 8 is a classic and beloved passage of engaging a life of worship in the Spirit of God. It's not just a passage about sanctification, but one in which we see the Holy Spirit bringing freedom from condemnation from any place the enemy seeks to bring the pressure of judgment upon a person because of sin.

"*There is therefore now no condemnation to those who are in Christ Jesus, who do not walk according to the flesh, but according to the Spirit"* (Romans 8:1, *NKJV*). This means as we learn this walk in the Spirit, there's no condemnation in the struggles we'll face. Instead, we'll come to experience both God's lavish grace for the process and His empowerment to overcome the darkness that ongoingly seeks to manipulate us. Paul's letter to the churches in the province of Galatia is as instructive to us today as it was to those who first read it. As believers, we are to *"Walk in the Spirit, and you shall not fulfill the lust of the flesh. For the flesh lusts against the Spirit, and the Spirit against the flesh; and these are contrary to one another..."* (Galatians 5:16-17a, *NKJV*).

Please understand, it's one thing to be delivered from the weight of judgment and condemnation because we have been born again through Jesus Christ and declared acquitted and righteous because of His Son. Still, it's another to be free from the judgments that hang over us. Sometimes these judgments result from our fathers' sins visited upon the third and fourth generations (*see* Exodus 20:5 and Deuteronomy 5:9). As we give ourselves to worship and walk the path of surrender in reliance upon the Spirit of the living God, many of our biological lineage's negative characteristics begin to fall away, and the nature of our heavenly Father begins to manifest in our lives.

At other times, the burden we carry is a residue of habits in our own lives because of the things we gave ourselves to and the way we walked in sin before we knew the Lord. As we come to learn the with-God life and abide in Christ, a new identity is developed in us, that of a son or daughter of God. We will begin to hear the Holy Spirit's whisper more clearly, "You are My beloved son." "You are My beloved daughter."

We grow to become more able to live our lives in the continual presence of the Spirit of God. We begin to walk in line with the Holy Spirit along the path He lays before us (*see* Galatians 5:25). It is a path of freedom that will leave our defeated spiritual enemies in our wake, for it is our Spirit-filled walk that welcomes God's majestic rule into our circumstances.

"Walking in and maintaining a thankful heart of worship in the Spirit brings a process of deliverance and freedom,"[38] the power of which is the honor and glorious privilege of all His people (*see* Psalms 149). The reality of the power of worship to release us is clearly demonstrated in the account of the deliverance of God's people under the leadership of Moses as he responded to God's commission, "Bring My people out of Egypt to this mountain that they may worship Me" (*See* Exodus 3:12). Israel discovered God's purpose and His key to their destiny in the power of His Spirit through their worship. "The way of deliverance—of unshackling their future—was not so much an open sea as an awaiting mountain. There they would hear from God and there come to know Him as they worshiped Him according to His will and His way."[39]

Before we move on, I offer one last point to remember about our Spirit-filled worship of God. It is much more than singing a song. While music is most assuredly a wonderfully significant element of our worship, it is not the only element. I've heard it said that to worship

---

38 Jack W. Hayford, *"The Multiple Means of Deliverance."* Lecture delivered in The First World Congress on Deliverance, Colorado Springs, CO. April, 2000.

39 Jack W. Hayford, *Worship His Majesty* (Waco: Word Books, 1987), 77.

the Lord is to center our mind's attention and our heart's affection on God. Worship is our every moment, all-of-life response to the worth of who God is and all that He does. As followers of Christ, we are charged to worship Him in Spirit and in truth as we walk out our lives with Him (*see* John 4:23-24). There, in His presence, we will find freedom, release, and the fulfillment of Almighty God's purpose and intention.

To worship is to center our mind's attention and our heart's affection on God.

The stream of authoritative prayer.

Yet another pathway to freedom from the snare of the enemy is the word and counsel of our authority in Jesus Christ. The command, "In the name of Jesus, come out!"

A read through the Gospels clearly reveals throughout His life on earth, Jesus ongoingly confronted the demonic and cast them out (*Among many examples, see* Matthew 8:16,32; 12:28; Mark 1:25; 5:8; 9:25; Luke 4:35-36; 8:2,29). As real as God's people came out of the slavery and oppression they lived under in Egypt, God has given His people today His authority in Christ to stand against the enemy and demand the hosts of darkness to come out and leave us.

It's a prayerful confrontation of Truth and the power of God, whereby a word of authority is spoken. Filled with Divine authority and power, our words become effective weapons against the forces of darkness. It is nothing less than the reality of the Kingdom of God come to the kingdoms of the world in which we live, as revealed in Jesus' declaration,

"But if I cast out demons with the finger of God, surely the kingdom of God has come upon you" (Luke 11:20, *NKJV*).

Confrontational prayer for deliverance employs the Holy Spirit's action and addresses the enemy in Christ's authority, not our own. It is a command attended by God's glory, which He astonishingly delegated to us, His disciples. It moves with the Holy Spirit's Divine power, the same Holy Spirit that raised Jesus from the dead (*see* John 17:22 *and* Romans 8:11).

And so we see that the ways God brings victory over the darkness are varied, and I'm confident that I've not yet discovered all of them. *"For My thoughts are not your thoughts, neither are your ways My ways, declares the Lord. For as the heavens are higher than the earth, so are My ways higher than your ways and My thoughts than your thoughts"* (Isaiah 55:8-9, *ESV*). Some of my most delightful and transformative times in prayer follow my question, "God, will you please tell me something about yourself I don't yet know?" Thus far, He's never run out of things to say! Incredible, isn't it? However, there will always be one thing common to each of His strategies for our freedom, and it's this, the matchless love of God will attend every pathway to deliverance.

In the chapter that follows, we'll spend some time dispelling another of the enemy's weapons against humanity, that of ignorance. Together, let's rise and meet the challenge of the Apostle Paul, to become familiar with the schemes of darkness, that Satan will not deceive or outmaneuver us. Are you curious? Read on.

CHAPTER NINE

BE NOT IGNORANT

"So that Satan will not outsmart us.
For we are familiar with his evil schemes."

(2 Corinthians 2:11, *NLT*)

Though we should not fear our enemy, Paul reminds us that we are wise not to underestimate him and to respect his power. As we engage in spiritual warfare, ignorance can only result in extreme vulnerability. In the words of Martin Luther, "On earth is not his equal," but as we've been learning, when we're on Calvary's ground, through the blood of Jesus Christ, armor securely in place, and the weapons of spiritual warfare God makes available to us implemented, we need not be afraid.

Satan is more than a personal name for the devil; it is a description of his character and his conduct—an opponent, an enemy, the false accuser, slanderer, the adversary who obstructs, hinders, and opposes, the hateful enemy of God, man, and good (*see* Job 1-2). He was a member of the heavenly hosts before his rebellion and fall and referred to as "...*Lucifer, son of the morning*" (Isaiah 14:12b, *NKJV*). His name signified a "light-bearer," revealing his prefall splendor as the "shining one."

Animated by his unrelenting hatred of God, the New Testament identifies Satan by his purpose and activities. He's described as "*the tempter*" (*see* 1 Thessalonians 3:5, *ESV*), "*Beelzebub, the ruler of the demons*" (Matthew 12:24b, *NKJV*), the "*evil one*" (*see* Matthew 13:19,38, *ESV*), and "*the ruler of this world*" who will "*be cast out*" (John 12:31, *ESV*).

Our adversary is also referred to as the "*god of this world [who has] blinded the minds of the unbelievers*" (2 Corinthians 4:4, *ESV*), "Belial" (2 Corinthians 6:15, *ESV*), "*the prince of the power of the air*" (Ephesians 2:2, *ESV*), "...*the great dragon ... that ancient serpent who is called the devil and Satan, the deceiver of the whole world*" (Revelation 12:9, *ESV*). We know him to be "...*a liar and the father of lies*" (John 8:44b, *ESV*). He most assuredly is our "*adversary ... like a roaring lion*" (1 Peter 5:8b, *NKJV*), "*the Destroyer*" (Revelation 9:11b, *NLT*), and "*the accuser of our brothers and sisters*" (Revelation 12:10b, *NLT*).

While this book's scope does not permit us an in-depth study, Ezekiel 28:11-19 provides us with a concise picture of the factors that led to the fall of the king of Tyre, one who was destined to carry out God's plans and purposes. This passage equally reflects the fall of Adam, Satan, and any proud human being for that matter. Most assuredly, Satan was magnificent in his created condition and position. The prophet Ezekiel speaks of his grandeur and his weakness, *"Your heart was proud because of your beauty; you corrupted your wisdom for the sake of your splendor."* (Ezekiel 28:17, *NKJV*).

Satan repositioned himself to center, rejecting God's moral guidance, subsequently developing a host of negative character traits to justify his decision. He rationalized his rebellion by blaming God and has raised suspicions about God in the minds of others ever since. The justice of God's character required Him to pass judgment on Satan, and *"...he was thrown down to the earth, and his angels were thrown down with him"* (Revelation 12:9b, *ESV*), becoming evil spirits, or demons.

There are multitudes of ways that Satan and his hosts of evil play out their tactics. Yet, upon closer examination, we see he repeats just a handful of strategies with minor variations to fit the circumstance. The devil has never had to change his tactics, either in heaven or on earth, because, unfortunately, they're still effective.

> **The devil has never had to change his tactics, either in heaven or on earth because, unfortunately, they're still effective.**

Looking back to the Garden and the temptation of Jesus, we observe several key similarities. Satan begins his deception against Eve by questioning God's Word and planting seeds of doubt in her mind. *"Did God really say?"* (Genesis 3:1, *NLT*). The temptation of Jesus also centered on raising doubt of God's Word (*see* Matthew 4:1-11 *and* Luke 4:1-13).

Satan's next attack was waged against Eve's trust in God's character (*see* Genesis 3:5) as he painted a picture of a god whose intentions were self-serving and withholding of freedom. Similarly, Satan challenged Jesus to turn the rocks into bread to satisfy His hunger, tempting Him to trust in Himself instead of trusting God's character and provision.

In essence, this describes the all too common human sin of autonomy—a self-governing independence that diminishes trust and weakens relationships, often leading to rebellion. It presents itself when we want to take matters into our own hands and handle things in our own way, instead of consulting God, trusting Him, and submitting to His voice.

Next, Satan convinced Eve that God's purpose could be accomplished by means other than God's (*see* Genesis 3:5-6). Satan also tempted Jesus with his extraordinary claim that he would give Jesus the kingdoms of the earth and authority over them if Jesus would worship him (*see* Luke 4:5-9). It's important to note here that Jesus does not challenge the claim, thus confirming Adam and Eve's disobedience forfeited their God-given position of rulership to Satan. Unlike Adam and Eve, Jesus puts an end to the temptation by speaking truth, "*You shall fear the Lord your God and serve Him*" (Deuteronomy 6:13a, *NKJV*).

God's intention was always that humankind would reign and have authority over the earth. "*The Lord God took the man and put him in the Garden of Eden to tend and keep it*" (Genesis 2:15, *NKJV*). Then, because God's created beings believed the enemy's lie—the lie that said God's purposes could be accomplished in perhaps an "easier, more practical" or "better way," God's intention for His creation was interrupted. But thankfully, because of the Father's great love for us, all was not lost.

Satan's tactic is a practical, matter-of-fact way of approaching or assessing the situations we commonly find ourselves in. It plays out in our lives in many ways, each time we make choices and decisions or attempt to solve problems based on our own reason and for our own benefit, without consulting the Word or the guidance and wisdom of the Holy Spirit.

Next is Satan's well-known strategy of pride. He told Eve, *"You will be like God" (see* Genesis 3:5, *ESV).* I ask you, does this remind you of something Satan desired for himself? To Jesus on the pinnacle of the temple, the most public of places, the enemy said, *"If You are the Son of God, jump off! ... [God] will order His angels to protect and guard You..."* (Luke 4:9-10, *NLT).* Jesus refused to give place to pride, responding instead with the Word, *"You must not test the Lord your God"* (Luke 4:12, *NLT, see also* Deuteronomy 6:16). Leaning on God's truth, He attacked the heart of Satan's proposition. A leap from the temple would have placed God in a position of being compelled to act. Jesus chose instead to humbly submit to God's timing and the revelation of His purpose.

Pride falsely believes one can manipulate God. Encapsulated in these events, we see Satan's overarching schemes and strategies, those that have been clearly identified by the Apostle John as three spiritual dynamics that he defines as the world's system. *"Do not love the world or the things in the world. If anyone loves the world, the love of the Father is not in him. For all that is in the world—the desires of the flesh and the desires of the eyes and pride in possessions—is not from the Father but is from the world"* (1 John 2:15-16, *ESV*).

Satan appealed to Eve based on these same desires. We see the lust of the flesh, *"the fruit was good for food;"* the lust of the eyes, the fruit was *"a delight to the eyes;"* and the pride of life, *"the tree was to be desired to make one wise"* (Genesis 3:6, *ESV*).

Satan again repeated this same pattern as he tempted Jesus in the wilderness. The lust of the flesh, *"command this stone to become bread"* (Luke 4:3, *ESV*), the lust of the eyes, as *"the devil took Him up and showed Him all the kingdoms of the world . . . will all be yours"* (*see* Luke 4:5-7, *ESV*), and the pride of life *"in front of everyone, show that You are God . . . jump off the temple"* (*see* Luke 4:9-11, *paraphrase, mine*).

These three temptations embody the heart of Satan's strategies. He threw his favorites at Eve, and they worked. He tried it again with Jesus, who, empowered by the strength of God's Spirit and His Word, did not yield,

The lust of the flesh, the lust of the eyes, and the pride of life ~
These three temptations embody the heart of Satan's strategies against humanity.

Yet, we're reminded the triumph of Christ in the wilderness would be a victory only for a season. *"And when the devil had ended every temptation, he departed from Him until an opportune time"* (Luke 4:13, *ESV*). The devil would be back to engage in battle again. From the time of his fall, Satan made his intention clear; it was *"to make war on the rest of her offspring, on those who keep the commandments of God and hold to the testimony of Jesus"* (Revelation 12:17, *ESV*). Beloved, again I remind you, as followers of Christ, this refers to you and me.

These battles also show us our adversary will use the Word; he will distort it and try to make us doubt its truth or doubt the character of the Author of the Word, God himself. Our enemy will design one plan after another to get between believers and their Bibles. Don't let him! Know the Word, commit it to heart, have faith in the Word, and, following the direction of the Holy Spirit, use it in prayer in the battles you face daily. Most assuredly, the Word of God is the decisive weapon in spiritual warfare.

The Word of God is the decisive weapon in spiritual warfare.

Satan's tactics with non-believers focus on keeping them from God's kingdom. He enslaves them, seduces them, addicts them, and discredits Christians in their eyes, just to name a few of his schemes. He then brings hopelessness, rejection, rebellion, anger, greed, idolatry, mistrust, lust, and rationalization. Our adversary is relentless in his attacks against unity, always seeking to divide. These are just some of the strategies Satan employs to accomplish his primary goal—to get people's eyes off of Jesus, believers and non-believers alike.

The devil also wages more subtle tactics against followers of Christ. He suggests we deserve more than others, a belief that opens the doors of entitlement, selfishness, self-will, and pride. He plants seeds of fear and draws us into the secrecy of darkness, deceit, and concealment. Our adversary whispers thoughts of doubt, self-righteousness, and overconfidence, including the idea that "just this once" or "just a little bit won't hurt." We understand seeds bear the fruit of their kind. Just as a peach seed will not produce an apple tree, we cannot afford to entertain the falsehoods the enemy whispers to us. Instead, identify them as the lies they are and eradicate them with truth before they bear the fruit of darkness.

Dear reader, remember we are stepping into the enemy's territory, the hateful one who comes to rob, kill, and destroy (*see* John 10:10). Demon spirits may be afforded entry by our various reactions and responses to the wounding each of us experience in daily life. The reactions of our flesh versus those of the Spirit, such as rejection of self, God, or others, bitterness, anger, fault finding, judgmentalism, addiction, fear, etc., are sinful in nature and not in alignment with God's will for the lives of His people. These attitudes fuel sinful actions and allow our enemy to torment us (*see* Romans 8). God's Word compels us as believers never to glibly blame the devil for the sin we yield to in carnal disobedience but to repent and receive His forgiveness.

This is by no means an exhaustive list of Satan's strategies. As much as we study his schemes, we still cannot truly know what is going on without the revelation of the Holy Spirit. When we guess, simply based on our experience or attempt to construct and follow formulas, we do ourselves a grave disservice and cripple our ministry efforts.

Without the Holy Spirit, we play into the enemy's hand, and we do not bring glory and honor to God. We must always lean into the Holy Spirit and ask Him for revelation. "Lord, show me by Your Spirit what's *really* going on here." God is so very faithful to answer that prayer, for He does not want us to navigate this battle without His wisdom and perspective. When we follow the Lord's directives, speak what He speaks, and do what we see Him doing, our victory over the darkness is assured.

Moving on, let me share some additional observations about Satan's kingdom as it compares to the Kingdom of God. It's critical to recognize that Satan is a created being, with derived and limited power, existing in time. God is the creator of all, including time itself. He lives outside of time, and His being is eternal, *"from everlasting to everlasting, You are God"* (Psalm 90:2, *NKJV*). God is the great "I AM" (*see* Exodus 3:14 *and* John 8:58), the everlasting now, without beginning or end.

All-knowing, or omniscient, our God is the bearer of all of the riches of knowledge and wisdom (*see* Job 36:4; 37:16 *and* Romans 11:33-36). He knows the past, present, and future, and the thoughts and motives of every heart cannot elude Him (*see* Psalm 147:5 *and* Hebrews 3:13). Satan cannot read our minds, though he wants us to think so, nor does he know the hearts of man. He only knows the thoughts that he plants, and he then keenly observes our responses and behaviors to them.

The devil is by no means passive. He will stubbornly refuse to leave the places in us we have surrendered to him until we, by God's power, cast him out.

But God! God the Almighty (*see* Genesis 17:1 *and* Matthew 28:18) is unlimited in His power (*see* Genesis 18:14). Also referred to as omnipotent, there is nothing He cannot do. Additionally, there is nothing our all-powerful God does that is inconsistent with His will, purpose, and nature. God's glory and the greatness of His majesty are made manifest in all He does. Such is the vastness of our enormously powerful God.

God is present, *Yahweh Shammah* (*see* Ezekiel 48:35), present with His people *"always, even to the end of the age"* (Matthew 28:20b, *NKJV*). God's extraordinary promise of His omnipresence reaches to embrace us with the fullest expression of His love. We realize His sacred promise to Moses long ago, *"My presence will go with you, and I will give you rest"* (Exodus 33:14, *NKJV*), is the same assurance that He gives to His people today.

In an incredibly relational tripartite declaration, God proclaims, *"I will walk among you and be your God, and you shall be My people"* (Leviticus 26:12, *NKJV*; *see also* Revelation 21:3). God promises us His presence, identifying with us, and giving us an identity as His own. Indeed, it is the presence of God that makes us the people of God.

The presence of God makes us the people of God.

God desires us to be His agents. "He doesn't move through us because we are unique in gifting. We are afforded the privilege of partnering with Him when we are available and surrendered to Him."[40] We are His Body on earth, privileged to carry out His will.

---

40 Jack W. Hayford, Sermon presented at The Church on the Way, Van Nuys, California, on November 15, 1994.

As we conclude this chapter, I encourage you to take away two more simple points of understanding. First, Satan's predictability is a decisive edge in the spiritual war we engage in as followers of Christ. Secondly, our most significant advantage is the non-negotiable truth that God is on our side. He has equipped us and stands with us. Whatever battles we face, we know the ultimate outcome of the war—with God, our triumph is assured.

May it always be said of us as Jesus spoke of Himself, *"I have come ... not to do My own will, but the will of Him who sent Me"* (John 6:38, NKJV). Nothing more and nothing less, always remembering, *"He who calls you is faithful; He will surely do it"* (1 Thessalonians 5:24, ESV).

In the next chapter, we're going to consider the times in our life experience when we might be particularly vulnerable to darkness. And, if you're anything like me, in humility, we also need to have a look at the ways we can hinder, obstruct or delay God's desire for our freedom all on our own, without any help from the enemy.

CHAPTER TEN

COULD I POSSIBLY BE MY OWN WORST ENEMY?

"All of us used to live that way,
following the passionate desires and inclinations
of our sinful nature."

(Ephesians 2:3a, *NLT*)

Together we've discovered there are events and situations in our lives that give the hosts of darkness the right to influence and manipulate us. There are times demonic spirits are given a point of entry by our sinful thoughts, deeds, or actions. Yet this is our hope and assurance, no matter our sin, God's love and forgiveness meets us right where we are. Beloved, it's the place where mercy wins, for the love of God is greater than all our sins.

God's mercy meets us right where we are, the place where mercy wins.

Then there are times that we become vulnerable to the enemy's oppression through no intentional action of our own. These occasions often result from traumatic events, accidents, severe wounding or illness, abusive relationships, etc. There is no compassion or grace to be found in the kingdom of darkness. The enemy will seize every opportunity to assail us. Our response to these events is the decisive issue. Further, it is essential to remember no matter what the circumstance, the destructive influence of the realm of darkness in our lives can and will be broken by the love and power of Jesus Christ and the authority we have in Him.

And so we come in humility before the Lord. It doesn't matter where you're from, what you've done, or what's been done to you. God's presence is a safe place to let down your defenses, agree with God about the things He already knows about you and seek His freedom. There will never be a substitute for inquiring of the Holy Spirit for the revelation of the Lord's heart and His strategy to fulfill His intentions for your life. Without Him, we sadly forfeit His miraculous offer of freedom. With all of my heart, I believe we have access to as much of God and His power as we have faith to receive it. But there are times the mighty move of His Spirit can and will be hindered.

We have access to as much of God and His power as we have faith to receive it.

My friend, it's time to get honest with God. These are the moments when our spiritual victories may be a simple process, but not always an easy one. It's hard to look at our own shortcomings. Let me share another testimony that will emphasize the freedom that comes when we're willing to come out of hiding, repent and receive God's forgiveness. At the conclusion of a spiritual warfare conference I was teaching, a woman came to me for prayer. Her sadness was evident in the tears flowing down her cheeks as she spoke. At fifteen years old, she didn't have a driver's license yet. Many of her friends were driving, and it didn't seem so hard. Thinking it'd be fun to give it a try, she was confident she could take her dad's new car out for a spin and return it unnoticed.

Late one night, she quietly sneaked out of their house, into the garage, and slipped into the driver's seat of her father's car. When her eyes met those of her inquisitive seven-year-old brother peeking into the garage, she realized she must not have been as quiet as she thought. Not sure she could trust her little brother to keep the secret of her adventurous joy ride, she invited him to come along. Excitedly he exclaimed, "Oh boy, let's go!" and promised he'd never, ever tell.

Less than a mile down the road, in the darkness of night, a drunk driver failed to stop for a red light, violently crashing into the passenger side of their car. Everything went black after that. The next thing she remembered was waking up in the hospital in tremendous pain. As she began to recover, her parents knew they couldn't delay any longer and gave her the heartbreaking news; her little brother had died in the accident.

Days turned into months, and a dark cloud of guilt and shame grew deeper. Her family and friends knew the circumstances of the accident, but they couldn't bear to see her pain. Hoping to comfort her, they repeatedly said things like, "Honey, it wasn't your fault," and "There's nothing you could have done to prevent the accident." Deep within her heart, she recognized that wasn't true. Though she was not at-fault for the accident, she knew she had taken her dad's car without permission. Her disobedience was the reason her brother was in the car. Had it not been so, he would be alive. She came to believe the lie the enemy whispered to her heart—God would never forgive her.

This woman was now in her mid-sixties. Though she had received Christ as her Savior as a young child, she had lived her entire adult life bound by guilt, shame, and condemnation. This evening God was about to change everything. She confessed her sin, repented for her disobedience and rebellion, and for the very first time, received Jesus' forgiveness. We then agreed in prayer and cast out the evil spirits who seized the opportunity that dreadful night of the accident to ongoingly torment her.

Words cannot describe the look on her face as we concluded our time of prayer. The Lord had magnificently set her free. She was almost glowing. Tears continued to flow, now in worship and gratitude before the Lord, as He continued to lovingly heal her broken heart. In a matter of minutes, Christ lifted the enemy's dark veil of guilt and shame—one she had lived under for over fifty years. It was an astonishing deliverance from half a century of bondage. No longer relegated to the gloomy prison of the adversary, her steps carried her into God's marvelous light as she exited the auditorium that night.

Together, she and I experienced a glorious story of freedom. Yet, my heart was deeply saddened by the reality this precious woman of faith had lived hindered by the weight of guilt, shame, and condemnation for so many years. If only she had known what to do about the enemy who had plagued her. It's my prayer this will never become your story.

So let's begin by defining the word "hinder." It's commonly understood that to hinder is to cause delay, interruption, or difficulty, preventing us from doing something. Something that's a hindrance creates an obstacle or impediment in our lives. Clearly, this is not God's intention for us, especially as it concerns our partnership with Him in spiritual warfare!

It's possible to be hindered at any dimension of spiritual warfare as we pray for the nations, our churches, our neighborhoods, our families, or our own lives. Let's look under the hood of that and investigate some potential hindrances, the places where the enemy has a "legal right" to oppose us.

What do I mean by "legal right?" Simply this, where God's will is opposed, the adversary is given an open door or legal right to gain entry and influence us. It's a place the enemy and his hosts have a just claim. That door must be closed to see God's freedom come. The Word of God is clear; we're compelled to give no opportunity to the devil.

The following are some of the most common obstacles I've experienced; ways our path out of bondage into God's freedom can be interrupted. As with all of the principles I've presented thus far, there are no formulas, and this is not an exhaustive list. At each point, I encourage you to inquire of the Holy Spirit for revelation if these hindrances might stand in opposition to your freedom.

Unconfessed Sin

"For the wages of sin is death" (Romans 6:23, *NLT);* and *"If we claim we have no sin, we are only fooling ourselves and not living in the truth. But if we confess our sins to him, he is faithful and just to forgive us our sins and to cleanse us from all wickedness"* (1 John 1:8-9, *NLT).* Paul's instruction to the Church went beyond belief in God. He also taught that God's people are to *"repent of their sins and turn to God, and prove they have changed by the good things they do"* (Acts 26:20, *NLT).*

It's important to understand that confession and repentance are two very different things. Confession is stating or recognizing our sin and acknowledging responsibility for it. But God also asks us to repent, which is a turning away from the sin, accompanied by our heart and mind's commitment to never commit that sin again.

Will we sin again? Well, I don't know about you, but I know I have and will again. Humanity tends to hide from its sin, seek refuge in the darkness, or blame and justify. We observe these behaviors in Adam and Eve following their disobedience, and it continues in us today. Thankfully, as we've just learned, our Father God invites us to run to Him in humble confession and repentance and receive His faithful forgiveness when we do sin again.

Unforgiveness

In no uncertain terms, unforgiveness will keep you bound (*see* Matthew 18:21-35). I have observed no enterprise of evil rises to hinder God's release in our lives more profoundly than unforgiveness. The bottom line is this; freedom in Christ will never be experienced if we, unlike Christ, harbor unforgiveness, bitterness, and resentment in our hearts.[41]

Forgiveness is best understood as an act of release, *Aphiemi*, meaning to let go, let alone, to allow to leave, and let be.[42] Think of it this way, when one person sins against another, a debt is incurred. The offender is indebted to the offended. Simply speaking, forgiveness is an act of release on the part of the offended to cancel the debt they are rightfully owed. In Jesus' life, we see forgiveness as an action, not a feeling or an emotion, as our present culture often wrongly concludes.

To forgive is to let go, let alone, and let be.

Another often overlooked aspect of forgiveness in the biblical world is that it's two-dimensional. We repent and seek God for His forgiveness of our sin, and then we must also repent and seek forgiveness from those we have

---

41 My understanding of forgiveness as seen through the lens of Biblical context reflects my study, decades of pastoral ministry experience, the lessons I have learned throughout my seminary education and the related conversations with and writings of Dr. Leah Coulter as noted in her book, *Rediscovering the Power of Repentance and Forgiveness: Finding Healing and Justice for Reconcilable and Irreconcilable Wrongs* (Atlanta: Ampelon Publishing, 2006)

42 http://www.lexiconcordance.com/greek/0863.html accessed June 12, 2020.

hurt. For the follower of Christ, a life of repentance and forgiveness is not a suggestion; it's a command.

The author of Hebrews reminds us that the Lord Jesus, upon being seated at the right hand of God, as part of the new covenant with those who believe, declared, *"Their sins and their lawless deeds I will remember no more"* (Hebrews 10:17, *NKJV*). Jesus does not forget our sins; rather, when we come to Him in true repentance, He forgives and intentionally chooses not to remember. It is this same choice God asks us to make throughout our lives as well.

Unforgiveness will hurt you. It gives the enemy a foothold in your life from which you will not be set free until you forgive as the Lord forgave. I once heard it said, *"To hold on to unforgiveness is like drinking poison and hoping the other guy dies."* Most assuredly, if we are unwilling to extend love, grace, forgiveness, and release to others, our prayers will be hindered (*see* Matthew 6:14-15 and 1 Peter 3:7). "We may talk all we want about dominion over demons or seek to command them to come out in Jesus' name. We can try to right every wrong and heal every wound. But if we are bound or tied up in a self-imposed straightjacket of unforgiveness, we will compromise the 'grace flow' of the Spirit which alone can 'loose' Kingdom powers."[43]

Forgiveness focuses on the guilt of the wrongdoer, not on the wrongdoing itself. The wrongdoing is not undone, ignored, or wiped out; instead, the guilt resulting from the wrongdoing is removed. When someone has sinned against us and then repents, as followers of Christ, we have no option but to forgive. As we forgive others, Christ forgives

---

43 Ibid., Jack W. Hayford, *Penetrating the Darkness.* 139.

us. *"If you forgive those who sin against you, your heavenly Father will forgive you. But if you refuse to forgive others, your Father will not forgive your sins"* (Matthew 6:14-15, *NLT*). And how often are we to forgive the repentant offender? Jesus said, "seventy times seven" (Matthew 8:22b, *NKJV*), reflecting an infinite number (*see also* Luke 17:3-4).

You may be wondering, what about the person who has never repented, and perhaps never will? Will God bring justice on my behalf and heal me from the hurt and scars that are so often too deeply painful for words? The answer is a resounding "yes!" Forgiveness doesn't deny justice; it entrusts it to God.

Forgiveness doesn't deny justice; it entrusts it to God.

God asks us to release the "debt" to Him. To do so is to transfer the debt to the Lord and wait on Him to bring Godly pressure where it needs to be, on the offender's need for repentance (*See* Matthew 5:23-24). But as long as we refuse to release the debts owed to us by the offender, we hinder the intimacy of our personal relationship with God. I have often been asked, "But isn't this just letting the bad guy off the hook?" You bet it is! But be assured my friend, in so doing, you are placing the one who has sinned against you on God's hook, the One who is infinitely more capable and trustworthy to reach the heart of the offender than we are.

As I have previously noted, Jesus lived the life He intends for us to live. We are to forgive as Jesus forgives. This statement compels the question, how did Christ forgive when He walked the earth? What does His example look like lived out in my life? Simply stated, He forgave the repentant sinner for the wrongs they committed against Him, and those who sinned against Him without repentance He released to the Father in prayer.

Think back to some of Christ's final words on the Cross. He didn't say to the Roman soldiers who were viciously pounding the nails into His wrists, "I forgive you." His posture was prayer. He looked to God and prayed, *"Father forgive them, for they do not know what they do"* (Luke 23:34, NKJV). He was releasing the debt owed Him by those brutal men to the Father. This act of prayer and release aligns with Jesus' earlier instruction to *"Bless those who curse you. Pray for those who hurt you"* (Luke 6:28, NLT).

We are called to revoke our right to revenge, retaliation, or justice, and give our debts to our justice-making God. The Lord commands us, *"Beloved, never avenge yourselves, but leave room for the wrath of God; for it is written, 'Vengeance is mine, I will repay'"* (Romans 12:19, NRSV). "The shocking truth is that God does not forgive the guilty unless they repent. God will judge injustice and bring justice to the sinned-against. Whether that justice comes in this age or in the age to come—He will not forget!"[44] God's vengeance is never vindictive; it is a loving justice-making act.

Like the woman's story I shared at the beginning of this chapter, there is also the reality that we may have refused to receive God's forgiveness for our own failures. More often than I wish to admit, I've believed I so profoundly let God down that I was undeserving of His forgiveness and

---

44 Ibid., Leah Coulter, 60-61.

love. It isn't so much that I've not forgiven myself; rather, I've resisted fully receiving the forgiveness Christ offers me. Can you relate? It's a price Jesus gave His life for you not to pay, and with my whole heart, I encourage you to receive His immeasurable gift.

Here's one more crucial issue. Forgiveness does **not** always mean reconciliation. These are two very different matters. If you are rightly releasing an unrepentant abuser or forgiving a repentant abuser from the hurt, wounding, or pain you have sustained as a result of their unacceptable behavior, yet the relationship would be unsafe for you to enter into again, God does not ask that you do so. At times, reconciliation can be accomplished as the repentant offender surrenders his or her heart to the healing and restorative work of God and is often facilitated in conjunction with professional counseling and a season of recovery and accountability.

For a deeper understanding of biblical repentance and forgiveness, I recommend reading the insightful book entitled *Rediscovering the Power of Repentance and Forgiveness* by Dr. Leah Coulter. She explains this truth far better than I can. Therein I know you will find a pathway to healing and justice for both reconcilable and irreconcilable wrongs and the often resultant hurt and deep wounds in your heart.

Unbelief

Unbelief will obstruct the miraculous power of God as we engage in spiritual warfare. We've covered the nature and consequences of unbelief in an earlier portion of this book. If you'd like, take a few minutes to go back and review Chapter 4.

Pride

"Pride goes before destruction" (Proverbs 16:18, *ESV*). The Bible deals harshly with pride, it being a severe hindrance to our spiritual life and freedom.

But God—because of His great love for us, furnishes us with a directive for how we can monitor the pride that seeks to enslave our hearts. *"Search me, O God, and know my heart; test me and know my anxious thoughts. Point out anything in me that offends you, and lead me along the path of everlasting life"* (Psalm 139:23-24, *NLT*).

Ultimately, pride will hinder victorious spiritual warfare and lead to outright rebellion against God. Pride is the very thing that seduced Satan into his rebellion against the Almighty (*see* Isaiah 14 and Ezekiel 28). Two of the greatest temptations in life are pride and self-exaltation. Our vigilance against pride and our commitment to maintaining a humble heart before God will most assuredly be one of the hinges upon which the door to successful and effective engagement in spiritual warfare will swing.

Idolatry

There's no nice way to say it; idolatry is an ugly thing, one that encompasses a vast spectrum of bondage in the human experience. It will often rise in opposition to one's personal freedom in Christ. We risk giving place to the sin and hindrance of idolatry anytime we look to something other than God for our identity or comfort.

Whatever we put above God, anything that takes His rightful place in our lives is an idol. It may not be a statue or a tree as in ancient times; it can be a system, a preference, or a pursuit that opposes God's rule and His will in our lives. A relationship, search for fame, our reputation, a hero, a job, a belief, a hobby, security, or any number of material things often lead us into the sin of idolatry. Surrender to occult involvement, promiscuity, drugs, alcohol, or pornography, etc., all give place to the devil, leaving us vulnerable to the sin of idolatry. Without question, idolatry will hinder us from experiencing God's magnificent power, deliverance, restoration, and grace in our lives.

As we conclude, I pray you will seek the revelation of the Holy Spirit, asking Him to expose any place that God's magnificent power and glory in you is hindered or obstructed. May you come before God in repentance and discover the cleansing love and healing of Jesus Christ in dimensions perhaps you've never known before.

In the chapter that follows, we'll engage a model for deliverance prayer. Together we've learned that we always pray with sensitivity to God's voice, direction, and timing. Scripture informs us through Jesus' ministry, there are no formulas for prayer, yet as you'll see as you read on, there are principles.

You may be assured of this, "God has not called us to be people who cope. He has called us to be people who conquer."[45] Nothing can keep you bound without your permission. Are you ready to come to Jesus and apply what you've learned? If so, prepare your heart, for you

---

45 Jack W. Hayford, *Penetrating the Darkness*. (Grand Rapids: Chosen, 2011), 127.

may be assured the victorious overthrow of your adversary and new dimensions of freedom awaits. Freedom that you may have perhaps never imagined possible.

> **"God has not called us**
> **to be people who cope.**
> **He has called us**
> **to be people who conquer."**
>
> *Dr. Jack W. Hayford*

CHAPTER ELEVEN

DISCOVERING THE FREEDOM THAT FLOWS FROM CALVARY

"You were dead because of your sins and because your sinful nature was not yet cut away. Then God made you alive with Christ, for He forgave all our sins. He canceled the record of the charges against us and took it away by nailing it to the cross. In this way, He disarmed the spiritual rulers and authorities. He shamed them publicly by His victory over them on the cross."

(Colossians 2: 13b-14, *NLT*)

By Christ's shed blood on the cross, He triumphed over the authority of all rulers and dark powers in Satan's realm.

The Word of God provides a simple, practical strategy to victoriously apply His triumph to the challenges the adversary throws at us in hopes to keep us bound. In childlike faith, we'll engage a Scriptural prayer model of repentance, renouncement, and breaking. Then, we'll seal the delivering move of the Spirit of God by welcoming His restoration, healing, and filling of the places vacated by the enslaving works of our common enemy, all for God's glory.

We begin with repentance addressing the specific sin we've engaged in, that for which we come to Him for freedom. There are two steps on this pathway: first, to acknowledge and confess our sin, and then turn away from sin. When we repent, our posture is prayer, for we are speaking to our loving Father God.

Like forgiveness and release, repentance is a decision, not a feeling. Repentance is not merely regretting or an apology; it's changing our thinking and our actions. To repent is to turn away from sin, disobedience, or rebellion and turn back to God (*see* Matthew 9:13; John 5:24; Luke 5:32). True repentance brings "godly sorrow" for sin, leading to the action of turning around and going in the opposite direction. It will result in a fundamental change in a person's relationship with God and with others. You may be wondering, but how can I know if I've fully repented? The answer is simple, when presented with the opportunity to sin again, you choose not to.

Our next step to freedom is renouncement. We read in 2 Corinthians 4:2, *"But we have renounced the hidden things of shame."* To renounce means to give up a claim, to cut off, and to refuse further association. In repenting, we tell God we are sorry, and we make the intentional decision, with

God's help, "to stay on the right path from now on. When we renounce, we go a step further by not only turning away from sin ... but by actively turning against it."[46] We reject the sin and the spirits of darkness that accompany it and declare we will no longer believe or make agreements with their lies. When we renounce, we are speaking directly to our enemies in the realms of darkness. Our posture is war.

Then, by the authority Christ has given us and in the power of His name, our next step is to break the chains that have held us in bondage. We dismantle the strength of any negative words, curses, or vows we have spoken or have been spoken over us. Any associations with ungodly or secret societies and unholy soul ties involving family, friends, and past sexual partners are severed. Hear the words of the prophet Isaiah, *"It shall come to pass in that day, that his burden will be taken away from your shoulder, and his yoke from your neck, and the yoke will be destroyed because of the anointing oil"* (Isaiah 10:27, NKJV).

The anointing of God does not diminish, nor does it merely weaken the influence of the enemy who enslaves us; it destroys it!
Thank You, Lord!

Our pursuit of freedom from Satan's grip brings us then to the place where we apply the Cross's provisions in Holy Spirit-empowered prayer and cast him out. Jesus declared, *"These miraculous signs will accompany those who believe: They will cast out demons in my name..."* (Mark 16:17, NLT). When addressing a demon, it is not recorded that Jesus

---

46 MacNutt, Francis, *Deliverance from Evil Spirits: A Practical Manual* (Grand Rapids: Chosen, 2009), 219.

ever prayed and asked the Father to "please take this evil spirit from this person." He directly rebuked the demons, commanding them to be quiet, to come out, and to go (*see* Matthew 8:32; 17:17-18; Mark 3:24-27; 5:7-13; 7:29-30; 9:25; Luke 4:33-35; 8:29-33; 9:42; 13:10-13,16). As followers of Christ, this is the very same authority He has given to us, for He has declared, *"Behold, I give you the authority to trample on serpents and scorpions, and over all the power of the enemy. . ."* (Luke 10:19a, *NLT*).

Follow the leading of the Holy Spirit, implement the spiritual weapons of warfare God has given you, and incorporate the power of His Word as you pray. There is tremendous power in speaking God's Word over your life. For example, "I speak the blood of Jesus over you spirit of darkness. In the matchless name of Jesus Christ, I lay the axe to the root of this bondage, destroy your hold over me, and command you to leave me now."

Are you ready? Let's do this! I'll ask you to repent, renounce, break, and fill, then step into God's glorious freedom. I can use almost any topic to teach the principles of prayer for our freedom in Christ, so I've chosen something I've struggled with more often than I'd like to admit, and perhaps you have as well; the destructive power of anger in our lives. As we seek freedom from anger, it's essential to understand what anger is and get a clear vision of what we want to accomplish.[47] We must

---

47 The late Dr. Dallas Willard's many writings, teachings, and lengthy conversations provided me with the fundamental principles I will share with you about the way anger works in our lives. He was a tremendous blessing in my life for which I will be always grateful. It is now my privilege and honor to pass a measure of his wisdom and insight in this area on to you.

begin by learning who we are in order to learn who God wants us to be.

Our overriding vision for life as a follower of Christ may be said to be, *living in the Kingdom with Jesus, manifesting His character and His power.* His character and His power go together, and both are needed to live out what is referred to as His Sermon on the Mount (*see* Matthew 5). If you have that vision, you will hear what Jesus meant when He says, for example, *"The old law said, do not murder, do not kill anyone; but, I say to you..."* (*see* Matthew 5:21-22). He then sets forth a sequence of teachings about how we are to regard people.

Now, this comes down to some particular things, and Jesus begins by addressing anger and contempt. At times I've wondered, why would He pick these two issues up first? As I began to observe relational conflicts, I soon realized anger and contempt are at the root of more evil than anything else in human life.

Consider with me, if you got rid of anger, how many murders would you have? I suggest very few, perhaps only those for the insurance money. I invite you to pause for a moment here and envision how good it would be to live without anger and contempt. Be assured; this alone will reorient ordinary life. You'll enjoy transformed relationships within your family, your church, your friends, and business dealings, basically, with everyone you encounter in day-to-day life.

Some of you might be thinking, "Well, then I couldn't stand for what is right!" Oh my friend, you most assuredly can stand for what is right without getting mad. Actually, I'm confident you'll discover that you will be much more effective if you refuse to express your position in anger. The truth is, anything you can do with anger, you can do better without it! In the climate of unrest and division we currently experience in our nation, it's clear to see when people get caught up in anger, they evoke anger in others, and then off the storm goes. As anger moves to the forefront, the concern people attempt to address quickly gets lost in the background.

Anything you can do with anger, you can do better without it.

Then, as anger progresses, people get caught up in their own self-righteousness. We often hear people talk about "righteous indignation." But I ask you, have you ever heard of any unrighteous indignation? Everyone who's angry tends to think it is righteous! For you see, it's the nature of anger that in the moment you think you're right. In fact, if you pull that out of it, you'll discover there's very little anger left. So God is calling His people to learn how to stand for what is right without getting angry. Lately, I've had people tell me, "Maureen, if you are not mad about the way things are, you're brain dead." I suggest to you this is precisely the attitude that has brought our world to the grievous state of being overcome with anger and contempt.

Moving on, engage this vision—that of the goodness of living without anger so you can effectively live in the Kingdom of God, manifesting His character and His power. The next step is to set your intention and make the deliberate choice to realize the vision—to live without anger and become a loving person. Understand, if you do not have a clear vision, your decision won't be stable. Beloved, you will never drift into it! You have to decide to do it! The clearer your vision and the goodness of it, the more stable your decision will be.

Now, there are many people who, if you would say, "I have a pill here, and if you take this pill, you will never be angry again," would decline your kind offer. Why? Because they have built their lives around anger and use it to manipulate and control people and circumstances. The enemy has deceived them into believing they need anger because what would happen if they lost control? Could they even survive without anger?

Unforgiveness is a form of anger, as are bitterness and resentment. Anger is the disposition to hurt, and that's why you're already mad if someone is mad at you. I don't even like to be honked at, do you? So, we see anger has an insidious way of building. The fundamental truth is, anger will rise to the surface whenever your will is crossed.

No matter how trivial it is, if you're a "self-willed" person and your will is crossed, you will become angry. May I encourage you to honestly think about how you respond if you get interrupted, if things don't go your way, or if you don't get what you want when you want it. When their will is crossed, the self-willed person always comes out in readiness to strike back.

Anger is a force for evil. It's not in itself a bad thing. It's an alarm that goes off, much like pain. Anger alerts us as it says, "Something needs to be changed," and that's a good thing! But as a follower of Christ, it's something you need to lay aside as a way of life and not sin in your anger.

Anger is only safe to the extent that when it happens, you are in control of it; it's not in control of you.

Once again, this is an intentional decision each person will need to make, that this is the way you want to be. Then, when it comes to carrying out your intention, you need "means," the method God sets forth for His followers to overcome anger victoriously.

The first pathway is in teaching; you have to learn what anger is. It's my sincere hope that this is what we've accomplished in our discussion thus far. Remember, anger comes because your will is crossed. I'm confident you'll discover that you no longer need anger when you surrender your will to God.

When Paul instructs us to lay aside anger, wrath, malice, and so on (*see* Ephesians 4:31), we must ask ourselves, how do I lay aside anger? By laying down self-will as the principle of your life. And how can you do that? Only by knowing God has accepted you, He loves you without measure and always has your best interest in His heart and mind. It's the settled assurance that He is in charge of your life, and then letting Him do that! I've discovered when you've got that thoroughly settled in your heart and mind, you'll be ready to let go of anger and pray to break the hold the enemy's spirit of anger has used to manipulate you.

You'll come to realize that if the plans you had for your day get interrupted by someone else's need, it's God giving you an opportunity to be a blessing to that someone. Or, if you get delayed in traffic, perhaps God intends to provide you with a moment to reflect on your day, or He very well may be protecting you from an accident up ahead, any number of things.

My friend, it all comes down to trust in Him and the surrender of your will to His. Just like Jesus did in the Garden on the eve of His crucifixion as He prayed, "...*nevertheless not My will, but Yours, be done*" (Luke 22:42, *NKJV*). It's surrendering a life-style of being a self-willed person. So our pathway to freedom begins with not just knowledge of how anger works but also a more profound understanding of God.

Back to anger. When a spirit of anger is exposed, at times, we get defensive and say things like, "I don't get mad, sometimes I just get frustrated." Compassionately, I suggest that frustration is just a sophisticated, more socially acceptable expression of anger. Or, you may have heard some people say, "Well, Christianity is about love, and I am a loving person." I'd have to ask this person, "How do you behave in traffic, or when you're hungry and tired?" Most assuredly, your circumstances have a way of ultimately revealing the places that you've given the enemy a foothold in your life.

Your family history also comes into play as you seek God's freedom. Like me, you may have heard people say things like, "Everybody in my family has a bad temper; it's just the way we are." Beloved, it's not the way God created you to be, and He loves you too much to leave you this way. Give heed to His Word: "*I lavish unfailing love to a thousand generations. I forgive iniquity, rebellion, and sin. But I do not excuse the guilty. I lay the sins of the parents upon their children and grandchildren; the entire family is affected—even children in the third and fourth generations"* (Exodus 34:7, *NLT, see also* Numbers 14:17-24).

God not only gives us permission to repent on behalf of our generations before us, but He compels us to do so. Then, when we do, He promises to remember all the blessings of His covenant and prosperity in the land He gives us to occupy. *"But at last my people will confess their sins and the sins of their ancestors for betraying me and being hostile toward me ... Then I will remember my covenant with Jacob and my covenant with Isaac and my covenant with Abraham, and I will remember the land"* (Leviticus 26:40-42, *NLT*).

Admittedly, most of us don't even know all the names of our great great great grandparents, let alone their sin and the many ways they may have betrayed God and His word. But know this, their sin will hinder the blessings God intends for you and your family to enjoy. You have the authority to draw a line in the sand, a line of Christ's shed blood to separate the sins of your forefathers from you and your family. In His name, you have the authority to declare the influences of darkness end today. It's now up to you to decide—will the legacy you leave be one of sin's bondage or the lavish blessings God promises will attend your family for a thousand generations to come?

At this point, the defenses that rise against pursuing God's freedom most often originate from the darkness itself. Be assured, the demons never want to leave you. They enjoy manipulating your life, and they want you to protect them by denying their existence. Our loving God has a better way for you to engage in life.

Sadly, you may also notice that when you've been angry and sinned by fiercely lashing out at people, it's usually the people you're closest to. With this behavior, you've regretfully given the enemy an open door to enter your life. The remedy Jesus provides is to cast out the spirit of anger. God's deliverance will end the enemy's legal right you've given him to manipulate you. It's freedom that brings you back to choice.

I also want to say a few words about fear, for fear and anger will often go hand in hand. As we know, anger is often used to control people or circumstances, and this is where fear steps in. We fear what would happen if we were to lose or give up our control. The sin of most fear is "mistrust," and like anger, it is also rooted in the unbelief that God loves you, cares for you in your present circumstance, and has your best interest at heart. Fear whispers, "You believe God can set you free, but will He? Probably not."

Fear can also gain influence in our lives through a crisis or traumatic event. Please hear my heart; there's no sin in that. But as I've discussed in the previous chapter, the enemy takes advantage of our vulnerability nonetheless. Then, we begin to believe and partner with his sinister lies, and off it goes. God's Word assures us this is not His intention for us, *"For God has not given us a spirit of fear, but of power and of love and of a sound mind"* (2 Timothy 1:7, NKJV).

One more thought before we pray. You may have heard some frightening, crazy stories about praying for deliverance. I encourage you not to let fear use those stories to stop you short of God's freedom. I promise you, as you pray, your head isn't going to spin around, and you won't vomit green slime.

The word for spirit in Scripture's original text is *pneuma* (Strong's 4151) and means breath. The demons enter with a breath, and they leave the same way. Some people I've prayed for cough as the spirit leaves, again, with a breath. Funny story—one time, a woman I prayed for did expel a rather forceful breath loosening her upper denture, which then went flying across the room. Thankfully, she had a delightful sense of humor and said, "That's OK, devil, I don't need my false teeth to tell you to leave me!" We laughed together and jumped right back into prayer. Moments later, she was miraculously set free by the breath of the Holy Spirit as He filled her with new dimensions of His life. Months afterward, I saw her and she mentioned she was glad it happened the way it did, for she was reminded of God's glorious gift of freedom each time she put in her denture.

Since the enemy cannot read your mind, please speak these prayers out loud. There's no need to shout, the demons aren't deaf, but they do need to hear you declare you're taking back the power you had once surrendered to them. Let's put this all together and get free from the whole dark mess!

We begin with repentance. In this segment of prayer, you are speaking to God Himself.

> *Father, I come humbly before You and repent of*
> *turning from the truths of Your Word, and in so doing,*
> *I acknowledge that I've given place to a spirit of anger.*
> *I repent of partnering with anger to manipulate, control,*

and hurt people. I repent of giving place to the spirits of darkness that work alongside anger; those of rage, violence, rebellion, any form of witchcraft, unforgiveness, bitterness, resentment, and anything else, known or unknown to me that has partnered with anger to enslave me to my volatile temper. I don't need all of the evil names, for I know The Name that is above every name, the name of Jesus Christ, and it's in His name that I come to seek forgiveness. I repent of all ungodly generational ties in my family's lineage with anger and all of the spirits of darkness that have collaborated with it. Please, forgive me, Lord.

I also repent of giving place to a spirit of fear and the spirits of mistrust and unbelief that conspire with fear to keep me from living a life of faith and trust in You, God. I am deeply sorry, Lord. I ask that you wash me whiter than snow, and I thank You now for the promise of Your cleansing blood. I humbly and gratefully receive Your forgiveness, Lord.

Take a deep breath and pause to reflect for a moment as you receive the vastness of Christ's loving forgiveness. I encourage you to express your gratitude and give Him glory.

Now we move on to renouncement. Remember, your posture now is war. As we continue, your prayer will seem repetitious. And it is. Because now you're no longer speaking to God; you are speaking directly to the spirits of anger and fear and all of their evil companions. You're putting them on notice that you'll no longer allow them to carry you off into the storms of their rage or partner with their lies. Continue boldly in prayer:

Father, by the authority You've given me as your blood-bought child, I speak directly to and renounce you, demonic spirits of anger, rage, violence, control, rebellion, witchcraft, unforgiveness, bitterness, resentment, and any other spirit, known or unknown to me, that has partnered with anger to imprison me and the generations before me. I further renounce the spirits of fear, mistrust, and unbelief. I assert, never again will I make agreements with you or allow you to manipulate me. I will not partner with your evil lies. I refuse all association with you and will resist you with all of the power of the Holy Spirit that my God moves through me. Never again will I permit you to speak through me to hurt and wound another person. Aligning with Psalms 139, verse 21, I declare that I hate you with a perfect hatred, and from this day forward, I count each of you my enemies.

Once again, take a few moments here to relax. Take a deep breath before we continue in prayer, and in confidant expectation, know God is about to set you free!

Praying aloud once again, break the power of the darkness.

In the matchless name of Jesus Christ, from my position of authority seated with Him in the heavenly realm and by His unrivaled power, I bring you, evil spirits, to Calvary's ground. Those of anger, rage, violence, control, rebellion, witchcraft, unforgiveness, bitterness, resentment, and any other spirit, known or unknown to me, or in the generations before me that have partnered with anger to enslave me to my volatile temper. I break your destructive hold over me. According to Your Word, Lord, I declare everything raised against me from the realms of darkness, everything contrary to God's purposes in me, has been taken out of my way, having been nailed to the Cross. I ask You, Lord, please take the hurtful effects of every word I have spoken in anger and heal the hearts of those I have wounded.

I further declare to you, spirits of fear, mistrust, and unbelief, your power over me is destroyed. By the strength of Christ's precious blood, I break every legal right, assignment, ungodly tie, plan, curse, or incantation originating in the realm of darkness as I uproot and destroy the hold you've had on me through the generations before me that has robbed me of the fullness of life my Lord and Savior Jesus Christ has intended for me. I declare that I am a blood-bought child of the living God. My heritage and the legacy I will leave for generations to come are rooted in Your goodness and faithfulness, Lord. From this day forward, I choose to walk only on Your path of life. Thank You, Jesus, that You have opened the prison doors and broken the chains that have snared me and kept me bound for so long. Thank You for the assurance that I am free, for it is written, "Therefore if the Son makes you free, you shall be free indeed" (John 8:36, NKJV).

Whom the Son sets free, is free indeed

And now, one more important step—let's continue in prayer to God Himself ~

Lord, You taught us, "When an unclean spirit goes out of a man, he goes through dry places seeking rest; and finding none, he says, 'I will return to my house from which I came.' And when he comes, he finds it swept and put in order. Then he goes and takes with him seven other spirits more wicked than himself, and they enter and dwell

there; and the last state of that man is worse than the first"
(Luke 11:24-26, NKJV). Aligning with this Word, I come
before You, cleansed by Your blood, and ask that You fill
every place in me now vacated by the darkness with Your
peace, Lord. Fill me with a calm, forgiving heart, fully
surrendered to You.

Lord, I ask You to reveal to me every person I need to
go to and not merely apologize, but also to ask for their
forgiveness for the ways I have hurt or wounded them with
my angry words or actions. I promise You, Lord, I will
follow through. Please go before me and prepare their hearts
to receive my repentance and extend forgiveness. Give me
Your heart of compassion and humility to love and serve
others. Fill me with trust, belief, and a greater measure of
confidence in the vastness of Your love for me. I love you,
Lord, and once again, thank You for setting me free. May
my life glorify You. In the name of Jesus Christ I pray,
Amen.

I ask that you pause once again and give God all the glory.
"Jesus, I rejoice in the freedom You have just given me. Thank
You, Lord, that You have freed me from the darkness of the
enemy's grip and ushered me into the freedom You purchased for
me at the Cross."

Beloved, I promise you, the enemy will whisper to you
later today, if he hasn't already, "Nothing happened just
now. That was way too easy." Refuse to believe your
adversary's lies anymore. If you sincerely repented and
prayed these prayers with the intention of being free and
living free, the spirits of darkness have bowed their knees
and fled. They had no choice. Yet still, you may ask, how
can I be sure? Because God's Word declares it! *"Therefore,*

God elevated him to the place of highest honor and gave him the name above all other names, that at the name of Jesus every knee should bow, in heaven and on earth and under the earth, and every tongue confess that Jesus Christ is Lord, to the glory of God the Father" (Philippians 2:9-11, NLT).

The enemy also loves to come with attempts to work in our minds to worry about semantics (possession, oppression, influence, etc.); we need simply to *"submit to God. Resist the devil and he will flee from you"* (James 4:7, NKJV). You may be tempted to wonder, "But, I didn't feel anything come out." I have to ask you, "Did you feel it come in?" Most likely not.

Again, you can be confident of your new freedom because God has declared it to be so. When the enemy comes with arguments such as these, simply say to him, "I am free because my Father has determined it to be so. So, Satan, if you have a problem with it, go talk to my Dad." As a child, did you ever hear anyone say to a bully, "My dad's bigger than your dad?" Now it's your turn to say that to Satan and his wicked hosts! Of this you can be sure; your Daddy God is bigger than any giant of darkness! Keep your eyes on the deliverer, Jesus Christ, and never focused on the demonic.

As with all deliverance the Lord provides, this day, He has ushered you "out of" and "into." You have stepped into a new realm, *"...that you may proclaim the praises of Him who called you out of darkness into His marvelous light"* (I Peter 2:9b, NKJV). As real as God's people were delivered out of the bondage of slavery in Egypt and into His promised land, you too have been delivered this day.

Will there be more enemies God will set you free from in the future? Yes indeed. Remember, there were giants in the land of God's promise. Empowered by God, His people went to war against them and victoriously conquered. Past deliverance will never remove all the giants from your future, for your freedom in Christ is a journey. While your salvation occurred in a moment, Jesus then set you on a path of life and freedom as He restores your soul (*see* Psalm 23:3). Day by day, He promises to transform you into His image, from glory to glory (*see* 2 Corinthians 3:18). In grateful response, give Him all the glory!

Today, remember you have fought the enemy not *for victory*, but *from victory*; Christ's victory on the Cross of Calvary. In so doing, God has victoriously brought you back to a place of unhindered ability to choose. Going forward, you will have the moments in which you'll be able to make the intentional decision not to respond in anger but to choose grace instead. You'll have the time you need to refuse the grip of fear and instead respond in faith to the circumstances around you.

Remember, the opposite of fear is not courage; it's faith and trust in our trustworthy, faithful God. You must guard your heart and mind as you align your thoughts with God's thoughts, "*casting down arguments and every high thing that exalts itself against the knowledge of God, bringing every thought into captivity to the obedience of Christ*" (2 Corinthians 10:5, *NKJV*).

**The opposite of fear is not courage;
it's faith and trust in our trustworthy,
faithful God.**

As we conclude this chapter, I remind you once again of the paramount significance of inquiring of the Holy Spirit for His direction and leading in prayer for freedom. The prayers you've just prayed serve as a model, not something you should write down and repeat with everyone you may be called upon to cast out the demonic spirits of anger or fear. Every person's circumstances are different. Jesus always listened for His Father's voice to lead and guide Him, and then He responded in obedience, *"For whatever He (the Father) does, the Son also does in like manner"* (John 5:19b, *NKJV*). We can do nothing less.

As we advance, the principles of repentance, renouncement, breaking, and filling can be applied as you pray for yourself, your children and grandchildren, or any other person God will bring to you. They will also be effectively used as you pray for God's freedom in your business, your neighborhood, your city, or the nations of our world.

Lastly, deliverance will never replace the need for obedience to God. As followers of Christ, it becomes our responsibility to maintain the freedom God has given us, and in the next chapter, we will discover the steps for us to take to do just that. In the words of John Ramirez, "In school, anyone can get an 'A' if they study; the grade is not the hard part. The hard part is maintaining the 'A.'"[48]

Deliverance will never replace the need for obedience.

---

48 Ibid., John Ramirez, 138.

Be encouraged. I remind you that Jesus did not leave you alone in this endeavor; He left you Himself, in the person of the Holy Spirit. For this fulfillment of the Father's promise, we praise You, Lord (*see* Acts 1:4-5). In the last chapter, I'll explain some of the ways God strengthens and equips you to victoriously live out the fullest measures of the freedom He gives you.

CHAPTER TWELVE

THE WARRIOR'S LIFE
OF FREEDOM

---

*"Stand fast therefore in the liberty by which
Christ has made us free, and do not be
entangled again with a yoke of bondage"*

(Galatians 5:1, NKJV)

In a moment, God miraculously sets us free from the
grip of the enemy. It pictures a prison cell having been
unlocked, the chains loosed, and the prison door, one that
may have been tightly sealed for many years, thrust wide
open. But living free is a life pattern. "It is depicted by our
standing up, walking out of that prison cell, and making
daily choices to walk the path of liberty and live in the
freedom bought for us at the cross."[49] Following God's

---

49 Ibid., Jack W. Hayford, *Penetrating the Darkness*. 124.

strategies to overcome the enemy's darkness, we are set free to pursue God's presence and boldly take His message of love and freedom to the world in which we live.

But here's what I have learned, we simply will not be successful in our efforts to live out our freedom, let alone share God's message of freedom with others, in our own strength. Most assuredly, we need the power of the Holy Spirit and God's unfailing grace as we walk the pathway He sets forth for us in His Word.

Paul opposes legalism, for it teaches righteousness in Christ depends upon our efforts and can be achieved by fulfilling a list of do's and don'ts. At the same time, however, God instructs us through the apostle to guard against sin, respecting the liberty, freedom, and grace the Lord extends to us. *"Stand fast therefore in the liberty by which Christ has made us free, and do not be entangled again with a yoke of bondage"* (Galatians 5:1, NKJV). We are not to return to our old ways. Again, our life experiences assure us this can only be accomplished by the power of the same Holy Spirit who empowered Jesus in the years He walked as a man among us.

If you prayed the prayers set forth in the preceding chapter, you'll remember in its conclusion, you asked the Lord to fill the void left by the departure of spirits of darkness with the Holy Spirit. Aligning with Christ's words penned in Luke 11:24-26, the prayer you have prayed has already begun to reverse the hazards and vulnerabilities of an empty life. Unfortunately, bad habits and the power of untamed desires remain, bringing questions like, "How do I maintain the freedom Christ has given me?" "How will I not give in to my weaknesses and the temptations to sin again?" Let's investigate God's Word for His Divine pathway.

Scripture unquestionably conveys our responsibility to align our will with God's. Isaiah 61 assures us of the joyous blessings and astonishingly good news Jesus Christ brings to our lost, oppressed, and hurting world. Set near the center of this portion of Scripture we read, *"They will rebuild the ancient ruins, repairing cities destroyed long ago. They will revive them, though they have been deserted for many generations"* (Isaiah 61:4, *NLT*). "They," not God! We must put our will in line with God's will. The responsibility to rebuild from the ruins of our poor choices and bad decisions is ours. God sets us free from the enemy's grip, releasing and empowering us to rebuild and repair the broken places that are the consequences of the adversary's cruelty.

"The primary source of our entanglement [with sin] is our desires—really, not just our desires themselves, but our enslavement to them and confusion about them. Temptation to sin always originates in desire (*see* James 1:14-15). We have set our hearts on too many different things, some of which are wrong or evil, and all of which are in conflict with some others ... and habitual following of a desire leads to strengthening the power of that desire over us."[50]

Scripture provides us with principles and disciplines of the Spirit. To walk in freedom, we must give careful attention

---

50   Dallas Willard, *Renovation of the Heart: Putting on the Character of Christ* (Colorado Springs: NavPress, 2002), 154.

to these principles and develop the disciplines with an attitude of heart that seeks God. Humbly come before Him, and *"Ask not for gifts but for the Giver of Gifts: not for life but for the Giver of Life—then life and the things needed for life will be added unto you."*[51]

I encourage you to remember as well, grace is not opposed to effort or to work. Grace is opposed to earning. Effort and work are actions, while earning is an attitude. It's wrong for us to think for even a moment that we can earn God's grace; it is His gift, offered freely to His people. God made it clear when He said, *"Without Me you can do nothing"* (John 15:5b, *NKJV*). We're wise to consider the inverse perspective as well, "If we're doing nothing, it's without God." God gave humanity a place of responsibility within creation, with His authority, to *"work it and keep it"* (Genesis 2:15b, *ESV*). Simply stated, we bear a significant measure of responsibility to maintain our freedom in Christ.

Become a person of praise, thankfulness, and worship.

Scripture compels us to express praise to God. *"Let everything that has breath praise the Lord!"* (Psalm 150:6, *NKJV*). Take a moment right now and do a quick check. Place the palm of your hand softly over your mouth and then breathe in and out. Did you feel your breath on your hand? All right! Now you know this Scripture is talking to you! One way to begin is to share with others the miraculous work of freedom God has done in your own life, for His Word affirms that we overcome Satan by the blood of the Lamb and the word of our testimony (*see* Revelation 12:11).

---

51 Sadhu Sundar Singh, 1889-1929.

Praise, thankfulness, and worship are not something we observe. Each of these actions is our heart's response to our remarkable God and is to become the essence of who we are. Worship is our twenty-four hours a day, seven days a week, all of life response to God, to acknowledge and value who God is and all He has done. We recognize the magnitude and glory of His character and His conduct, His acts, and His being in gratitude for the vastness of His love for us.

Become a person of the Word.

Listen to the Lord's instruction to Joshua as He commissioned the young warrior to lead His people across the Jordan River into the land He gave them, *"Study this Book of Instruction continually. Meditate on it day and night so you will be sure to obey everything written in it. Only then will you prosper and succeed in all you do"* (Joshua 1:8, *NLT*). If we intend to prosper and succeed in life, we need to live close to Jesus and regularly engage His Word. Jesus is the Word! (*see* John 1:1,14). The truth we find in the Word of God sets us free (*see* John 8:32).

To sustain our freedom, continue to discover more, and be equipped to engage the war between the Kingdom of God and the kingdoms of this world, we simply must align our everyday lives, thoughts, and actions with the truth of God's Word. *"Your Word is truth"* (John 17:17b, *ESV*), and we thank You, Lord, for this powerful reality.

To use the Word of God as a filter through which you consider all of your thoughts is a habit that must be cultivated. You may be assured of this; your thoughts will inevitably lead to your actions. I urge you to begin to think about what you're thinking about! To maintain the freedom God has given you personally and become an effective spiritual warrior, it's vital to engage the discipline of choosing "our own thoughts rather than letting the devil fill our minds full of things that will destroy us. We must learn to be responsible for our thoughts and words because they produce our actions. It is impossible for us to behave better unless we think better thoughts."[52] Read and meditate on the truth of God's Word daily, and let Him renew your mind as He fills your thoughts with His.

> ## "Don't copy the behavior and customs of this world,
> ## but let God transform you into a new person by changing the way you think"
> ## (Romans 12:2a, *NLT*).

Walk in the Spirit.

Paul encourages us to understand, if you walk in the Spirit, you will not fulfill the lusts of the flesh (*see* Galatians 5:16). In other words, you will be holy because the flesh will no longer control you. We always have a choice, either to perceive circumstances through the filter of the flesh or the Spirit. Listen to the voice of the Spirit and be quick to respond. We are wise to walk in the fullness of the Holy Spirit.

Jesus commanded His disciples to wait until they received power when the Holy Spirit would come upon them. He knew very well they would need the fullness of the Holy

---

52 Joyce Meyer, *Battlefield of the Mind: Winning the Battle in Your Mind, updated edition.* (New York: Faith Words, 2011), x.

Spirit to complete all of God's purposes as they advanced the evidence that He is alive! (*see* Acts 1:8). And God has declared the promise of His Holy Spirit is for you as well. *"You shall receive the gift of the Holy Spirit. For the promise is to you and to your children, and to all who are afar off, as many as the Lord our God will call"* (Acts 2:38b-39, *NKJV*).

We know that the baptism with the Holy Spirit provides strength for the believer. *"That He [God] would grant you, according to the riches of His glory, to be strengthened with might through His Spirit in the inner man"* (Ephesians 3:16, *NKJV*). It is not my intention within the pages of this book to engage the debate regarding the baptism with the Holy Spirit or speaking in tongues, a topic that at times has caused tension and division within the Church for many years.

However, I will assert, if the supernatural ministry of Jesus is to be replicated in and through your life, He assures you as He did His disciples that His intention is for you to receive the power and enablement of the Holy Spirit (*see* Acts 1:5,8). As it concerns spiritual warfare, it is my firm belief and experience that to engage the unseen battle with the forces of darkness without the empowerment of the Holy Spirit and all of the fullness of His gifting would be comparable to stepping into a fierce military battle unarmed.

"The answer is simply to look at the example of Jesus, who walked with God for thirty years, then needed a new dimension of union with the Spirit to empower Him for ministry. I need that subsequent empowering too."[53] You

---

53 Ibid., Francis MacNutt, 279.

may remember that Paul, ministering to *"some disciples"* in Ephesus, inquired of them, *"'Did you receive the Holy Spirit when you believed?'* So they said to him, 'We *have not so much as heard whether there is a Holy Spirit.'"* Paul went on to confirm their repentance, belief in Christ Jesus and baptism in water, then *"laid hands on them, [and] the Holy Spirit came upon them, and they spoke with tongues and prophesied"* (*see* Acts 19:1-6).

I invite you, just for a moment, to set aside any preconceived notions or positions you may have and simply ask yourself if, since you have believed, have you indeed received the fullness of the Spirit, attended by all the diversities of gifts He makes available to us for ministry? (*See* 1 Corinthians 12:4-11).

Most assuredly, to move beyond the realm of our natural humanity and victoriously engage in spiritual warfare, we need the vibrant power of the Holy Spirit in the most extraordinary measure. The Spirit's gifts provide us with His infinite, supernatural resources of enablement to thoroughly equip us for the battle, and I believe it is wisdom for us to seek being filled with God's Holy Spirit. Will you trust Him moving forward?

The Lord wants to advance us in power and prayer. From Pentecost until our Lord's return, the Church's commission is to be *"endued with power from on high"* (Luke 24:49, *NKJV*), to *"do business till I [Jesus] come'* (John 19:13, *NKJV*), to *"go into all the world"* (Mark 16:15, *NKJV*), and to experience *"the Lord working with [you] and confirming the word through the accompanying signs"* (Mark 16:20, *NKJV*). "Fulfillment of this rather full mandate is only possible through being baptized in the Holy Spirit and continually being freshly filled with His love and power."[54]

God leaves the decision with you. If you have not been baptized with the Holy Spirit and sense that is something the Lord is calling you into today, I invite you to bow your heart with me and pray this simple prayer:

> *Dear Lord Jesus, I thank You and praise You for the vastness of Your love and faithfulness to me. My heart is filled with joy as I ponder the great gift of salvation You have so freely given to me. I come in humility and glorify You, Lord Jesus. I now also come in obedience to Your call. I desire the fullness of the Holy Spirit. Because You have washed me from my sins, I thank You that You have made the vessel of my life a worthy one to be filled with the Holy Spirit of God.*
>
> *I want to be overflowed with Your life, Your love, and Your power, Lord Jesus. I long to show forth Your grace, Your Words, Your goodness, and Your gifts with those I encounter every day. So, in simple childlike faith, I ask You, Lord, to fill me with the Holy Spirit. I open all of myself to You, to receive all of Yourself in me. I love You, Lord, and I lift my voice in praise to You. I welcome Your might, Your dominion, and Your miracles to be manifested in me for Your glory and unto Your praise.*[55]

If you have partnered with me in this prayer, you have invited Jesus to baptize and fill you with His Holy Spirit. Now, rather than concluding with an "Amen,"

---

54   Jack Hayford, *Living the Spirit Formed Life.* (Ventura: Regal, 2001), 116.

55   Ibid., Jack W. Hayford, *Penetrating the Darkness.* 187-188.

I encourage you to simply begin to praise and worship Him in faith. Allow the Holy Spirit to come and enrich your understanding of what He has done for you in these moments. Don't hesitate to be filled with the glorious expectation for the same things to happen in you that happened to His people we read about within the pages of Scripture. Magnify Him, love Him, trust Him, and then leave the rest to the Holy Spirit.

At your request, the Spirit of Truth has filled you; He whom Jesus promised will *"guide you into all truth; for He will not speak on His own [authority] but whatever He hears He will speak; and He will tell you things to come. He will glorify Me, for He will take of what is Mine and declare it to you"* (John 16:13-14, *NKJV*). Hallelujah!

Love the Lord and move toward Him in intimate fellowship.

Jesus' own words instruct us in this attitude of our hearts when He said, *"You shall love the Lord your God with all your heart, with all your soul, and with all your mind"* (Matthew 22:37, *NKJV*). To be ongoing in our walk in freedom and to be equipped for battle, we must continuingly seek to maintain intimacy in our relationship with Jesus. "If we want to do more by doing less, we need to get into God's presence [and] prayer is the difference between the best we can do and the best God can do."[56]

Peter is one of my favorite disciples; I think because I can relate to him and all the times he seemed to make mistakes and just basically "blow it." But Peter always took the risk

---

56 Ibid., Mark Batterson, 18.

and stepped out in faith, and even when the outcome was not as he had hoped, Jesus never failed to teach, encourage, and restore him.

Reading through the Gospel accounts, I was recently reminded when Jesus healed Peter's mother-in-law, Mark tells us that Peter's house was in Capernaum. John, however, mentions in his Gospel that Peter's hometown was Bethsaida. Bethsaida was a fishing village situated on the Sea of Galilee, an advantageous place for a fisherman to live. Scripture does not explicitly inform us when Peter moved his family to Capernaum. What we do know is that Peter moved away from all that was familiar and occupationally advantageous to him, to be closer to Jesus in the place the Lord lived after leaving Nazareth.

Consider another of Peter's moves toward Jesus. Following his denial of Jesus and Christ's death and resurrection, Peter was fishing with some of the other disciples. After a miraculous catch of fish, the men suddenly realized it was Jesus who had instructed them where to fish and was now on the shore inviting them to come and eat breakfast with Him.

At that very moment, Peter did not wait with the others for their boat to reach the shore. *"Now when Simon Peter heard that it was the Lord, he put on his outer garment ... and plunged into the sea"* (*see* John 21:1-7). Despite the sorrow he felt following his denial of the Lord, Peter once again made a move to be closer to Him. The result? It brought about Peter's repentance, the Lord's restoration, and the birth of Christ's call on Peter's life to shepherd His sheep.

Contrast these events with Judas's betrayal of Christ (*see* Matthew 26:20-25). Remorseful of his betrayal, he *"brought back the thirty pieces of silver to the chief priests,"* who refused to accept it. At that, *"he threw down the pieces of silver in the temple and departed, and went and hanged himself"* (*see* Matthew 27:3-5). Have you ever wondered what would Judas's life have been like if, instead of running away from Him, he had run to Jesus and humbly repented? I have. We know this much, Jesus would have forgiven and restored him, just as He did Peter, and as He does with us as well.

Do you now curiously wonder, what's the point of this comparison? Simply this, as we are faithful to move toward Jesus, seeking a close, intimate relationship with Him, no matter how we have sinned and fallen short, the result will always bring life.

When we move toward Jesus, the result will bring life. When we move away from Jesus, the result will bring death.

At this point I ask, you may have never physically moved away from Jesus, but have you ever drawn away from Him in your heart? When we move away from Him, either physically or emotionally, the result will be death. Perhaps not our physical death, but death all the same. It may take the form of death to hopes, dreams, or the fulfillment of our loving Father God's purposes and intentions for our lives. Beloved, always move toward Him in surrender to His Lordship. His promise is *"...a rich and satisfying life* (John 10:10b, *NLT*).

One of the most significant ways we accomplish intimacy with God is in prayer. I've learned that prayer doesn't change God; it changes the one who prays. Prayer involves speaking as well as in stillness and silence, listening. It's a conversation with the Creator of all heaven and earth, not merely in contemplation but in direct address to Him. I believe prayer to be a privileged pathway we walk on to draw near to God, one that Christ lovingly opened to us on the Cross. To be in prayer is most assuredly to *"dwell in the secret place of the Most High [and to] abide under the shadow of the Almighty"* (Psalm 91:1, *NKJV*). Above all else, we know this, *"It is good for me to draw near to God"* (Psalm 73:28a, *NKJV*).

Fear the Lord.

2 Corinthians 7:1 is about *"perfecting holiness in the fear of the Lord."* Fear means having a deep reverence and respect, an awareness of God's majesty and power. It's standing in awe of our Holy God and never losing our wonder. Sometimes we get caught up in Jesus being our friend, and we forget His majesty.

Here's a simple way to understand this. Let me ask you, "Do you fear electricity?" (By the way, you should—it can hurt you!) Or, "How about gravity? Do you fear gravity?" Now electricity and gravity are not mean, and they are not angry. They're just electricity and gravity.

I see the fear of the Lord like that. It is the humble acknowledgment that He alone is God and we are not. Therefore, we stand in respectful awe of Him, understanding that our very life and breath are in His hands. And, we want things to go His way, assured that it will always be the very best way.

"Fear of the Lord is the foundation of wisdom. Knowledge of the Holy One results in good judgment" (Proverbs 9:10, NLT). To fear the Lord is to acknowledge His absolute sovereignty and power. He is far greater than we can comprehend. One of my seminary professors once told me, "There are some things about God that are meant to be worshiped rather than understood." I believe God's majesty is an aspect of His character and nature that falls into this category. And so, to rightfully fear Him is to maintain a worshipful attitude of heart, one that wisely surrenders to Him in respect and reverent awe. It will be an attitude that will serve you well as you seek to maintain your spiritual freedom and live like the warrior God calls you to be.

Rejoice in your salvation.

Once again, think back to Luke's account of Jesus' disciples joyfully reporting their miraculous ministry success, *"Even the demons obey us when we use your name!"* (Luke 10:17b, NLT). Christ's response appears to be a warning, *"Look, I have given you authority over all the power of the enemy . . . but don't rejoice because evil spirits obey you; rejoice because your names are registered in heaven"* (Luke 10:19-20, NLT).

In essence, Christ was saying to them, "Don't rejoice in what you are doing; rather, rejoice in what I have done on your behalf. I love you, I have saved you, I died for you, and I chose you as My bride." While it's breathtaking to hear of the miracles the Lord is doing, the reality that Jesus chose to write your name in His Book of Life is enough to transform you into a joyous follower, ever grateful for His magnificent gift of love. To worship Him with a heart full of love, gratitude, and reverence is our most incredible honor and privilege.

Stand in liberty.

Jesus said, *"Go, and sin no more"* (John 8:11, *NKJV*). Always remember Jesus didn't leave you alone to fulfill this proclamation and overcome the evil enticement of sin. He left you Himself in the person of the Holy Spirit to empower you to love what He loves and to hate what He hates.

To walk in freedom and the strength of a warrior compels you to declare with the heart and passion of the Psalmist, *"Do I not hate those who hate you, O Lord? And do I not loathe those who rise up against You? I hate them with complete hatred; I count them my enemies"* (Psalm 139:21, *ESV*). It's a call to hate sin, completely and without compromise! Living in this truth, we realize God's promise still stands, *"Resist the devil, and he will flee from you"* (James 4:7, *ESV*).

To stand in liberty also demands that you carefully guard your words. Solomon, king of Israel warns, *"The tongue can bring death or life"* (Proverbs 18:21a, *NLT*). As God speaks, He decrees, and when He speaks, what He has said shall be. Being created in His image, you choose what you will give voice to. Your words will either come into agreement with God's Word or declare your agreement with the realms of darkness.

Do not give place to unforgiveness or bitterness.

Jesus taught that when we refuse to forgive those who have repented, we will be *"delivered to the torturers,"* and the enemy who will keep us in bondage (*See* Matthew

18:21-35). Remember, when you forgive the repentant sinner, it does not make what they have done right; it sets you free and releases God to heal and restore the wounds in your heart.

To come to the Lord for freedom from the adversary's grip is not the only time we are to be concerned with seeking and extending forgiveness. God calls us into a lifestyle of forgiveness and release. As a follower of Christ who desires to be transformed more and more into His image, we come to realize we are so greatly forgiven we truly have no option but to model His compassion and forgiveness. We are to remain ever watchful that no root of bitterness grows up to trouble and corrupt us (*see* Hebrews 12:14-15).

Live in the fellowship of believers.

As the people of God, we are the Body of Christ, one body, of which He is the head. In Acts 2:42, Luke tells us the early church continued steadfastly in fellowship. Jesus Christ has explicitly given gifts to His church *"for the equipping of the saints for the work of ministry, for the edifying of the body of Christ"* (Ephesians 4:12, *NKJV*). The gifts He gives are those whom He has called and appointed to be apostles, prophets, evangelists, pastors, and teachers (*see* Ephesians 4:7-16). When we don't engage the fellowship of believers, simply stated, we won't experience the benefits from the men and women God has anointed to serve His people in these offices.

Beloved, Jesus Christ loves His Church, so much so that He sacrificially and lovingly gave His life for it. Being the Church identifies us as *"the bride, the Lamb's wife"* (Revelation 21:9, *NKJV*), living in covenant union with Him. With that thought in mind, I encourage you to consider this truth; you cannot forsake the bride without forsaking The Bridegroom.

You cannot forsake the bride without forsaking The Bridegroom.

Remember that temptation is not bondage.

"The essence of all temptation is the invitation to live independent of God and fulfill legitimate needs in the world, the flesh or the devil instead of in Christ."[57] Our response to temptation always involves choice, one that is ours alone to make.

Know this, the most persuasive temptations the enemy presents often involve nothing extreme. They're subtle, and for a time may go unnoticed. Temptations unchecked become negative patterns and habits. Then, before we know it, we find ourselves bound by the chains of darkness.

Solomon, the wisest king to ever reign in Israel, observed something seemingly innocent could lead to a devastating consequence and warned, it's the little foxes that spoil the vineyards (*see* The Song of Solomon 2:25). We must remain keenly alert to the seductive lure of darkness and non-negotiable in our biblical responses to life's circumstances.

Guard your heart.

People have come to me for ministry and from time to time said things like, "I play with an Ouija board—it's no big deal though, it's only a game." Or, "I let my kids

---

57 Ibid., Neil T. Anderson, *Victory Over the Darkness*, 161.

read books and watch movies with sorcery and witches, but it's just fantasy, so there's no harm in it, right?" Some have participated in a séance with the intent of listening to a spirit medium or receive messages from the dead, thinking it was merely entertainment.

Here's what I've experienced, there's no dabbling in the realm of darkness. When you open the door, either a crack or throw it open wide, the enemy takes every opportunity to step in like a roaring lion. Nothing is a game to the deceiver. I encourage you to protect your heart and the hearts of those you love from any dimension of evil. King Solomon said it best, *"Guard your heart above all else, for it determines the course of your life"* (Proverbs 4:23, NLT).

People have sought supernatural powers other than God since the beginning of time. Your adversary will entice you to engage horoscopes, mediums, games, and occult practices to lure you away from God and into his kingdom of darkness. Your hearts are the essence of all you are and the source of everything you do. One of the ways to be vigilant in guarding your heart is to be discerning and alert to the devil's seductive tactics. What may seem harmless often camouflages the enemy's vicious attempt to lure you away from God (*see* Matthew 7:15). Hear God's instruction to His people, *"Do not defile yourselves by turning to mediums or to those who consult the spirits of the dead. I am the Lord your God"* (Leviticus 19:31, NLT).

Never let yourself be without a trusted friend/ counselor/coach; one who will tell you the truth,

knows you well enough to be frank with you without judgment, and will hold you accountable.

Once again, consider the words of King Solomon, who confirms that we sharpen one another, *"As iron sharpens iron, so a man sharpens the countenance of his friend"* (Proverbs 27:17, *NKJV*). We stir each other to goodness, to integrity, to the utilization of God's gifts, and to the expressions of His compassionate love. God created us to live in community, one with another.

Oh, how we need one another! Trust me; we are all blind to our blind spots! Renowned counselor and grief recovery expert Dr. H. Norman Wright once wisely cautioned me, "Always remember this, if you're the only one you're talking to, you're probably getting really bad advice." At first, I laughed but later realized how very true it is.

"If you're the only one you're talking to, you're probably getting really bad advice."

When you invite regular times of accountability with a trusted, mature person of faith, you grant them permission to help you become aware of your blind spots or encourage a shift or broadening of your perspective. When you love another, you earn the right to speak the truth. It's so much more than pointing a finger; it's holding out your hand to lift each other to a higher place.

I'm confident this is far from an exhaustive list; however, these endeavors are crucial to freedom and power in God's Kingdom. God longs to transform us, that we will become transforming instruments in others' lives, and our effectiveness will flow from these basics, either discovered or recovered.

"In the last analysis, our spiritual life is one of simple moment-to-moment dependence upon Jesus ... [and] no method, system or discipline will ever substitute for our just being His."[58] No discipline will remove us from the war with darkness, seasons of dryness, affliction, trials, or temptations, but they will always change us, and we determine what that change will look like.

There are truly no formulas that will enable us to "master" a spiritual warrior's lifestyle and live in the fullness of the freedom Jesus gave His life to provide us. It is an ongoing journey of drawing near to Him that we may become like Him. After having walked with the Lord for nearly half of a century now, I have only recently come to discover that to mature in my relationship with Him is really to become more and more childlike in my faith, keeping my eyes ever focused on Jesus.

Moving forward, may we accept the following glorious invitation from Him, the Fountain of Living Water, "*...the Spirit and the bride say, 'Come!' And let him who hears say, 'Come!' And let him who thirsts come. Whoever desires, let him take the water of life freely*" (Revelation 22:17, *NKJV*). It's in this place we will never thirst again (*See* John 4:1-14).

In the brief chapter that follows, I conclude our warrior's training out of Satan's darkness into the marvelous light of God's freedom with a story. It is a true story, the account of which I have entitled, *"In The Master's Hands."*

---

58 Ibid., Jack W. Hayford, 269

CONCLUSION

IN THE MASTER'S HANDS

"So we don't look at the troubles we can see now; rather, we fix our gaze on things that cannot be seen. For the things we see now will soon be gone, but the things we cannot see will last forever."

(2 Corinthians 4:18, *NLT*)

In the mid-1460s one of the world's most accomplished artists of the time, Agostino di Duccio was commissioned by the *Operai*, the Office of Works of the Florence Cathedral in Italy, to create a statue depicting the Old Testament figure of the warrior king David.

The massive block of marble Agostino was to use most likely came from the quarry of the Fantiscritti in the Miseglia district of Carrara, with the reputation of having marble used to create dozens of famous sculptures and buildings throughout the world. The artist failed to progress beyond blocking out the figure and drilling a hole where the space between the legs would be. Agostino abandoned the project late in 1466. The enterprise was resurrected some ten years later by a second artist whose contract was subsequently terminated without any real progress.

Unfortunately, the enormous, aged marble block, now determined by two sculptors to be filled with imperfections, riddled with brittleness, and aesthetically inferior veins running throughout, lay neglected in the courtyard workshop of Florence Cathedral for the next twenty-five years. The fractured piece of marble further deteriorated during its years of exposure to the elements, and countless pinholes riddled the surface.

Still hopeful of reviving the project, in 1501, the Arte della Lana, responsible for the upkeep and decoration of the Cathedral in Florence, approached a twenty-six-year-old artist whose first name was Michelangelo. Though relatively young, having just completed the stunning *Pièta* in Rome, he was recognized as a genius and determined to be a master of his craft.

Though binding decisions had already been made in the stone by the badly roughed out and forsaken attempts of the previous artists, the city fathers made clear to the spirited young sculptor, this seemingly useless and severely damaged piece of marble was too expensive to waste. It would indeed be the only marble he would be given to use to create the statue of David. Undaunted by the obstacles, Michelangelo envisioned a masterpiece and agreed to take on the commission in 1501.

It would be two full years until its completion. Michaelangelo tirelessly worked on the statue in near darkness and utmost secrecy. The outcome is the iconic statue of David, well known to be the perfection of a masterpiece and one of Florence's most magnificent sculptures, and perhaps, in all the world. Michelangelo's astonishing piece of art has blessed thousands upon thousands for centuries and continues to be admired to this day.[59]

At the hand of a master, the extraordinary was created from what the world had deemed less than ordinary. That which was hidden away in darkness was brought into the light, useless became priceless, worthless became treasured, cast aside became valued beyond measure, and fractured became whole. At the hand of a master.

In Paul's letter to the church at Ephesus, he writes, *"For we are God's masterpiece. He has created us anew in Christ Jesus, so we can do the good things He planned for us long ago"* (Ephesians 2:10, *NLT*). Beloved, it all comes down to trust. Our God is a trustworthy God, and He is faithful to complete all He has begun in you.

With His loving, masterful hand, God has formed you and will guide you, empower you and equip you. He will heal

---

59 Debra Thimmesch, "The History of Michelangelo's David Statue." Italiarail.com, April 20, 2020. Accessed on July 20, 2020. https://www.italiarail.com/culture/michelangelos-battle-il-gigante-story-behinds-italys-famous-david-statue. Together with https://www.michelangelo.org/david.jsp. Accessed on July 21, 2020; and https://www.italymagazine.com/dual-language/story-behind-michelangelos-david. Accessed on July 21, 2020

and transform you into the man or woman He created you to be. By the power of His Holy Spirit, the Lord of Heaven's armies will lead you to rise and assume your role in the Spirit to destroy the places the devil gained access to through times of vulnerability or sinful choices you've made. The enemy took advantage of those events as an invitation to influence, manipulate and hurt you, all with the intention of drawing your focus off of the Lord and onto your weaknesses, failures, and brokenness. But God!

Irrespective of any mistakes you have made, poor decisions that caused fractures, the deterioration of hope in your life, or the pain and wounding resulting from hurtful things others have said or done to you, when you entrust your life into the hands of The Master, His strength comes to bear on every shortcoming. His light shines through your weak, fragile, and broken places as He lovingly and tenderly restores your soul.

No longer will you interpret your present through your past, your purpose through your pain, or your future through your flaws. God will give you eyes to see yourself as He sees you. As you war in the spirit for your families, your loved ones' identities will no longer be interpreted through the opinions of others or their social media feeds. Media assessments will fail to diminish your hope for the Church and the nations of this world. Your faith will stand firm in the plans and purposes of our everlasting God, *"with whom there is no variation or shadow of turning"* (James 1:17b, NKJV).

Dear reader, this is what spiritual warfare is all about— the recovery of all that was lost and the redemption of all that the enemy has stolen. At the Master's hand, we are renewed, restored, and transformed once again into His image. By His Spirit, we are empowered and equipped to recover the position of rulership God intended for us to occupy before time began. On this side of Calvary's victory, we're able to confidently engage life and extend "the reach and dominion of God's Kingdom as surely as Adam and Eve were originally called to."[60]

As we conclude our journey together, will you bow your heart in prayer with me one last time?

> *I surrender to You, my Good Shepherd, who did not come to take me out of a fallen world but to empower me to victoriously overcome the darkness and corruption that is so pervasive. I have come to understand You intentionally designed me and have commissioned and equipped me to defeat the evil one as I impose Your work on Calvary into every situation in my life.*
>
> *Thank You that You have redeemed me from an empty way of living, as You continue to heal and make whole the places in my heart, mind, and emotions fractured by the shrapnel of a world gone terribly wrong. Bring me to a place of confident trust in You! Help me know You more deeply as the Shepherd and Guardian of my soul (see 1 Peter 2:25), assured of Your promise to keep a watchful eye over me.*
>
> *Lord, I invite Your Holy Spirit to shine His light on me and reveal any broken, dry, or fractured places, as I pray with David, "Search me O God, and know my heart, test me and know my anxious thoughts" (Psalm 139:23, NLT).*

---

60 Ibid., Jack W. Hayford, 45.

I welcome the Master's touch, recognizing that it is only Your hand that can restore and redeem the places in me that I have believed would remain broken forever. Thank you, Lord, that Your hands lovingly sculpt my life into something of immeasurable beauty and worth, reflecting You.

Thank you, Good Shepherd, that You became the Lamb and gave Your precious blood to pay the price to purchase my weak, imperfect clay vessel. Thank You, Jesus, that You have ransomed me from an empty way of life, and promise to graciously continue to form and shape me to bear Your glory.

And now, extend your hands with me as you continue in prayer.

Lord, I commit my hands to You, that I may respond to Your call to lovingly represent you with integrity and grace as an ambassador of Your Word. Anoint my hands anew this day, that mine will be hands that, when extended to others, will always convey and deliver Your touch of redemption, restoration, freedom, healing, and the vastness of Your love to a broken world.

Thank you for restoring my hope, Lord—hope for the future and my ongoing freedom. Hope for my children, my grandchildren, and the world in which I live. May I continually step into the fullness of Your intention and purpose, unhindered by the bondage of darkness. I entrust my life to You, Lord, the One who made me. May I go forward to victoriously accomplish the most extraordinary privilege that life will ever hold, that of stepping into the unique role that You created me exclusively to fill. In the mighty name of Jesus Christ my Lord, I pray, Amen.

I leave you with one last word of encouragement. Inquire of the Holy Spirit for His eyes to see that which the natural eye cannot see. Oh, not just the darkness, beloved, but more importantly, to see the magnificent, penetrating light of the living God that you may behold His glory. I am confident He will enable you to gaze into His eyes, the One who loves you with unfailing love, that you may begin to see yourself not as the world sees you, but as God sees you. For it is therein, you will find the warrior's strength and effectiveness for the days in which we live. And it is also the place where you will experience His perfect peace.

Thank you for the trust you've placed in me as you've navigated my book and the journey into the promises of freedom Jesus gave His life to provide. You've not come to the ending; instead, you've arrived at the beginning of a new chapter of God's story unfolding and lived out in and through you. May the ordinary events of life continue to be transformed into the extraordinary. As you continue to walk with God in the days ahead, I pray His most lavish blessings will attend all you set your hands to, by the matchless power of His name, Amen.

CPSIA information can be obtained
at www.ICGtesting.com
Printed in the USA
BVHW040602210523
664489BV00005B/104

9 781954 618121